Vision Of Truth

How Spiritual Realities Of Mankind Were Revealed To Me

Eagle Awareness Series

Book # 1

Kathy O'Connell

Vision Of Truth

Copyright © 2014 by Kathy O'Connell

All rights reserved. This book or any portion thereof may not be reproduced or used in any manner whatsoever without the express written permission of the publisher except for the use of brief quotations in a book review or scholarly journal.

First Printing: 2015

ISBN: 978-0-9962455-9-3

Published by Eagle Awareness Publishing
Sand Springs, OK 74063

www.Eagle-Awareness.com

Ordering Information: $15.99
Special discounts are available on quantity purchases by corporations, associations, educators, and others. For details, contact the publisher at the email listed below.

U.S. trade bookstores and wholesalers: Please contact Kathy O'Connell at Eagle Awareness Publishing

Email: kathy@www.Eagle-Awareness.com

Dedication

To my dearly departed husband and one
true Love, Larry O'Connell
and his sister, Doris Kline,
as well as my mentor and Indian
Grandmother, Jackie Morrow, who adopted me in
the Indian Way.

Thank you from the bottom of my heart.
Without your support and patience, I would
have never made it through all these years of
waiting.

Table of Contents

INTRODUCTION 7
THE GRAND CANYON 13
MY TRAVELS 41
    THE JOURNEY CONTINUES 42
    AUSTRALIA BOUND 53
SPIRITUAL CURIOSITY 67
    FINDING MY PATH 68
    SEEKING SPIRITUAL INSIGHT 71
    SPIRITUAL VISITORS 77
FINDING PURPOSE 89
    MY DIVINE PURPOSE 90
    THREE MESSAGES 92
    BACK TO AMERICA 100
    SEEKING MY DESTINY 102
    EAGLE AWARENESS 112
DESTINY ON TRACK 117
    EXPERIENCING KRYON 118
    JOURNEY TO THE RETREAT 123
BECOMING AN AUTHOR 139
    A BRIEF ENCOUNTER 140
    THE BOOK TO NOWHERE 153
DEALING WITH DILEMMAS 167
    MY SITUATION 168
    MIRACLES HAPPEN 177
    THE JOURNEY OF WRITING 188

A TURN FOR THE WORST ... 191
- Misunderstood Blessings ... 193
- A Handicapped Widow ... 195
- Rock Bottom ... 203
- Choosing Life ... 207
- Something Wasn't Right ... 209
- My Promise Was Fulfilled ... 213

THE REASON FOR EVERYTHING ... 219
- Discovering Solutions ... 219
- A Disguised Blessing ... 223
- The Law Of Love ... 225
- Love's Reason ... 226
- The Reason Is Love ... 232

A CALL FOR HELP ... 237
- Specific Needs ... 238
- The One Remaining Condition ... 241
- Another Scenario ... 244

REFERENCES ... 251

Introduction

Back in April of 2001, when I first set out to write a book in answer to a directive from Spirit, the world was a very different place. So different, that I felt deep in my heart the world was not ready for what I was being asked to write. Now, 14 years later, the world has changed, and is changing in ways I never imagined possible. I've wondered, all this time, what was taking so long for me to get the promised sign from Spirit (referred to as God by some) letting me know it was time to publish my book. Today I understand, it wasn't time yet, because the world wasn't ready, until now.

Even though most of what you are about to read describes the major spiritual phenomenon I've been through, my primary goal is to share with the world some remarkable truths regarding how the universe works. I was witness to some of the most important information the world has yet to understand about the reality we live in and the part we play in it. I'm alive today to reveal what I was shown during a profound spiritual experience of literally biblical proportion. Astoundingly, my journey of discovery didn't stop there.

My life has been a series of spiritual experiences, messages, visions and miracles for more than 42 years resulting in a huge spiritual jigsaw puzzle I've been trying to piece together since it all began. This new book actually started out as a way for me to sort out this jigsaw puzzle once and for all. I could have just shook my head and

Vision Of Truth

moved past it like most people do when something bizarre happens. In fact, I would have done exactly that, if it would have ended where it began on that fateful summer day when I was working as a Grand Canyon employee. That option became completely impossible for me by the sheer accumulation of spiritual episodes following that amazing experience outweighing anything I could possibly ignore.

How can a lifetime filled with endless overpowering spiritual events possibly have all been for nothing? That is what I've been asking myself lately, as I sit here in the latter years of my life more than 40 years since making a divine vow to share what I was shown with the world, and still the opportunity to fulfill that promise has not yet come to fruition. One thing is sure; it is definitely not due to my lack of trying.

Ever since the day I was shown the means, that I should write a book, I've done everything I could to achieve it. For over 12 years I worked diligently doing the in-depth research into the verses of the Bible using 5 dictionaries to do the word clarification required to write and rewrite the book I thought I was being directed by Spirit to write. All those years of effort to only be forced to let it go with the realization that it will never be published, at least not as a single book or as it is now written.

You may be wondering why I would dedicate that much time and energy towards something I didn't even try to get published. The answer is found in the story of my life, which describes not only how I know what I know, but why that should matter to anyone reading this. I am alive for this purpose alone, but for you to fully understand why I say that, or even what difference that should make to you, I

Introduction

have to tell you my story. I have quite a story to tell, as you will soon see.

This book is very different from the book I spent 12 years writing, which I've put aside for now. This is a completely new book, starting over from scratch with a concentration on my own spiritual journey, a spiritual memoir. Please realize, however, this book is much more important than anyone's individual story could ever be. It is a necessary beginning that will lay the ground work so I can finally expose what humanity needs to know in order to grow beyond our meek existence and embrace our next evolutionary step.

The only reason I am telling you my story is so you can discern for yourself the validity of the astounding information I am here to share. It should help you see, just as it became clear to me, that it couldn't have all been for nothing. This new, and what could even be shocking information for some, is not just coming from the imaginations of some unknown author. It is important for you to know how profoundly the realities of our world became known to me and how Spirit has literally driven me to this day. My story should help you realize that this information is coming from Spirit, not from me. I am only the vehicle.

Taking on a task in answer to a calling from Spirit is far from an easy job to fulfill, but I will continue the effort to stand by my promises for as long as I am able. With repeated efforts to perfect the book I was called on to write and constant expectations of divine approval being right around the next corner, all of which I explain here in detail, it is with great relief to finally begin to share what I've known for so many decades. This has been a waiting game that has worn me down until it felt like a cosmic joke that has gone on way too long.

It was less than a year ago, in my 60th year, as my physical handicap became overwhelming, when the hope of ever helping humanity through my work became severely diminished. Literally reaching the end of my rope, even knocking on death's door, I noticed something was starting to change in the world. People, it seemed, were able to hear me at long last. I can finally deliver the information I know will help humanity overcome the world, which gave me the drive to fight through my difficulties, another part of my story I explain in the pages to come.

I've been in a prison of isolation from the world with spiritual promises keeping me quiet for a very long time. As that prison door opens ever so slightly, I instinctively know what the world is ready to hear and what still has to be processed by the consciousness of mankind. Since there is more than can fit in any single book and way too much information for anyone to absorb in one sitting, I now know my news for the world must be put into a series of books. I'm calling it the Eagle Awareness series for reasons you will discover in this first book, since it was also spiritually decreed.

I am confident, as this new information is released through this series, that the prison door assuring my silence will open more and more. It's enough, for now, to know that I am able to share the most important new information of it all, the part that I promised to share on that fateful day and have been longing to shout out to the world since I was barely 19 years old. I am 61 now. It's been a very long wait.

Understand this above all else, I did NOT ask for this life. Who in their right mind ever would? It was never my

Introduction

goal to write a book or to become a spiritual teacher. I didn't even pursue a spiritual life, it pursued me! This series of books is my calling, to share with mankind the answers to many of the big questions humanity has been asking since the beginning of human life on earth. All I ask is that you open your heart and mind to my story and what you can learn from my journey. Even this first book will show you how to turn your life around for the better, since that is my primary purpose and will always be the main focus.

To really benefit from what I have to say, it would help you to leave your perceptions of religion and the way the world works behind you, just for this journey, please. There is one thing I can promise you right up front, that nothing, and I mean NOTHING, is as it seems. To assume the world is as it appears is the biggest mistake mankind has ever brought down upon itself. It's time to lift yourself up to the truth of our existence and fully understand your place in this new world and in the reality of all that is.

The Grand Canyon

Betz couldn't believe her ears, when her brother offered to take her out west with him in his newly revamped hippy van. Steve, being 5 years older than Betz (pronounced like the vegetable "beets"), had always pushed her love away with the cynical attitude that love just wasn't something their family did. She never understood that way of thinking, since it was obviously a choice he was making with every hug he shunned and with every complaint over the "charade" of any family time their parents tried to organize.

Her oldest brother, Gary, who gave her the unusual nickname, was gone off to college by the time Betz was only seven years old. Therefore, since their parents were too busy to care, Betz only had Steve as a distant hope for a supporting bond in her family. Steve rewarded her admiration with abuse, justifying his treatment by his belief that they were just not a close family. Betz knew, even from a very young age, that attitude would only lead to exactly what both of her brothers believed they already had, a family devoid of love.

That's why, when Steve asked her to join him on such a wondrous journey clear across the country, since they lived in Florida at the time, she was completely dumb struck by the offer. In truth, her brother's motivation for the invitation was more to strike back at his mother than to show love towards his sister, even though he really did want to help Betz escape the control their mother had over her.

All through school, every aspect of her life was under the controlling hand of their mother, often from the cold distance of secretly placing other people in charge of Betz. What her mother didn't take the time to notice was the after effect of her manipulations and demands. Unable to find any friends her mother would approve of, Betz was forced to play alone. She grew up intensely lonely and became the constant target of bullying at school as well as at home.

Even Sunday school was a source of frustration for Betz, since they seemed to teach more about fear than the love they claimed their God had for her. To her young mind, love and fear simply did not belong in the same sentiment. With it up to Betz to discern the truth, it was love she saw as the only authentic teaching. Betz insisted fear was not going to be her motivation to love, or even learn, about God. So, once she managed to fake her way through to Catechism, she wanted nothing more to do with religion or churches in her life.

Through it all, Betz developed a strong independent skin, while also fostering a deep-seated sense of compassion for the pain people inflict on others by mere words. Expecting the freedom to make her own choices would follow high school, she packed her bags to show support for her dad. Her mother had come through on her constant promise to end their marriage as soon as Betz was

The Grand Canyon

out of school, and kicked him out on the very same day she graduated with her class of '71. But her dad, the one example of compassion she was able to witness growing up, always remained in support of her mother, and couldn't allow it. When Betz saw the poor conditions her dad was forced to reside in, she understood why he didn't want her to join him.

Since school had always been a sore spot for Betz, and since she had never been encouraged to attend college, Betz didn't really have a plan beyond finding a job so she could get out from under her mother's rule. With no warning, she suddenly found herself in a car with her mother heading 250 miles north. She was being informed for the first time, as they drove, that her mother had already enrolled her in a beauty school and her bags were secretly packed and hidden away in the trunk of the car.

Having grown up as more of a "tom boy" than a "girly girl", the last thing Betz wanted to do with her life is become a beautician. With the promise of having her own apartment paid for, however, Betz gave in once again to her mother's controlling manipulations. It turned out, however, that the teacher at the beauty school was just another governing force placed in charge of Betz, who stayed in close contact with her mother.

Enough was finally enough, when she discovered the teacher was listening in on her lunch breaks through an intercom system. Betz found her strength when she showed up to school wearing a tie dyed T-shirt and a hippy headband across her forehead. She was announcing to the teacher and to the world that she wasn't going to be controlled anymore. Betz knew posing as a hippy, even though it didn't yet define who she actually was, would infuriate her teacher beyond belief, making her exit from school a huge splash fellow students would talk about for years. Problem was; it would also mean her free ride was coming to an end, which eventually forced Betz back home and once again under her mother's control.

Steve, having seen right through all their mother's manipulations from the start, since he had rebelled against them several years prior, could see that Betz was being sucked in for life by their mother's most recent plan. He had to step in when he saw Betz falling for the promise of a horse stable and a small parcel of land if she stayed there to develop it into a profitable business. Even though Betz saw no way to achieve that, her love for horses was strong enough to take on the challenge and see how far she could go with it.

Steve saw it another way, knowing his mother didn't do anything that wouldn't benefit herself. He realized the value of that land was going to sky rocket with the coming promise of a major development going in there. He knew the only thing their mother was doing is buying time in hopes Betz would meet a man who would keep the control system going strong. That's why he had to step in when he did, first by trying to point out their mother's true intentions.

Betz knew she was always getting the short end of the stick in their family, evidenced most recently by the used turn table she got as a graduation gift when both of her brothers had received a car. She was just so hungry for any expression of love that she would willingly accept whatever morsel they presented to her. She didn't want to believe her mother would pull that land out from under her if she were able to turn it into a profitable venture. Still, how do you turn a horse stable and a couple acres of land into a life sustaining income, especially when you were not being offered any capital to work from? She realized, her mother expected her to fail.

That's why, when her brother made the astounding offer to travel together, she jumped at the opportunity without hesitation. To Betz, first and foremost, it felt like she was finally being accepted by her favorite brother, like maybe he really did love her. Besides, a long journey out west sounded like an exciting adventure. She felt honored to even sit in his awesome van, much less be expected to drive it on occasion.

They headed out in April of 1972, while she was still only 18 years old, almost a year following her graduation from high school. They took their sweet time stopping every chance they got to take in the sights, since they were more interested in enjoying the journey than in reaching an undetermined destination. The sibling's recent common interest in their own American Indian heritage grew stronger with each stop along their westward journey. They went out of their way to locate the historic markers and visit the few Indian Trading Posts they found along the way.

Nothing enthralled them more than when they woke up somewhere deep within the Lincoln National Forest in New Mexico. Betz was already asleep in the back of the van the night before, when Steve pulled into the parking lot of a small picnic area to grab some sleep himself, so neither of them knew where they were in the dark. Their delight and surprise grew exponentially with each new discovery of the next day as they thoroughly explored Sitting Bull Falls.

The plaque at the guard rail designed to keep tourists away only enhanced their curiosity, with its story of an Indian Chief who made off with the livestock of a local rancher and disappeared at that point of pursuit by the cavalry. The falls, staring back at them from the plaque location, was a solid wall of water reaching about 15 feet across and at least 50 feet high, with the huge boulders on the far side of the falls enclosing the box canyon. Where could the Indians have gone to hide with livestock in tow?

They answered that question together, starting with their discovery of an unexpected avenue through the wall of massive boulders barely wide enough for a single horse to travel through leading to a small corral of more boulders. At the mouth of the avenue Steve noticed some small hand holds carved into the first boulder towering way over their heads. Situated just far enough apart for a person to grab from horseback, the hand holds would have provided a well hidden access to climb to the top of the huge boulder blocking the view of its hidden avenue, as their horse would have continued forward into the corral. Too difficult to reach the first hold from the ground, Steve found a way to achieve it by climbing the smaller adjacent boulders. What he discovered at the top gave Betz the courage to fight through the difficult climb to join him, where all their questions were answered.

Starting at the top of the huge boulder, an ancient hand carved stairway, which encompassed at least 20 steps, began its incline up the far side of the waterfall. It was positioned perfectly, where the splashing water edge would have covered the accent of the last stray Indian braving his way up the rock wall. The hidden stairway was a treacherous climb for Betz, since the many small steps covered with ages of moss were soaking wet in some spots and dangerously shallow from erosion in others. Steve, having reached beyond the last step, promised her the climb was worth it, as he stood just below the water spillway and behind the wall of water where he would have been visible only from this far side of the falls. He was

The Grand Canyon

encouraging Betz to join him from the opening of a massive cavern tall enough to easily stand erect and deep enough to fit 20-30 Indians and many more in the adjoining tunnels. The siblings stood there together marveling over the brilliant hiding place as they looked out at the perfect view their ancestors would've had of their pursuers through the one way picture window of water.

The discovery of an enormous underground lake of pure water housed within the walls of the cavern made their exploration a truly amazing find. This easy access to plenty of drinking water would have made it possible for the Indians to remain hidden there as long as it took for the Calvary to give up the search. The discovery of this amazing hideout was breathtaking for the siblings, as they sat behind the wall of water pondering how rarely others would have followed their footsteps of investigation. The only evidence of another human being ever finding it before them was a single steel Milwaukee beer can advertising the newly invented can opener tool, the ancient "church key", on its side. Steve took it with him, not only as a memento, but to clear the area of any and all human contamination.

Further exploration of the site revealed an even better lay out, when they found a narrow back door tunnel leading deep into the cavern and then up to above ground far beyond the view of anyone hanging below. Upon examination of those upper regions, it became clear that this reclusive spot had been used for some extended stays for many Indian braves and their families. They found several caves all charred by fire and some with ancient artwork gracing their walls.

After such an exhilarating day of exploration and discovery, their respect for their Indian heritage was at an all-time high. The siblings wanted to learn more, but were frustrated by their white skin and tourist aptitude. All they could do is observe from their forced distance as they tried to follow the example of their ancestors by exercising a reverence for their natural surroundings. They even established their own Indian-like ceremonial method of fire building, respectfully taking great care of the forest they camped out in every night of their journey.

Finally, they were accepted by one Indian as being a true relative when they picked up a Hopi Indian hitch hiker. On one long stretch of driving, their newly found brother taught Betz all about omens, on what to watch for, and how to interpret their meaning. He even invited them to his home, where he said his parents would welcome them as the brother and sister they were, since this is the Indian way.

He would have to join them there later, however, since he had to make a stop that would take him a few days. So, he wrote down a phone number they could give to his parents to confirm their intentions. With that precious piece of paper in hand, it was off to the Hopi Indian Reservation as quickly as their hippy van could get them there.

Steve was especially excited about their invitation to the Hopi Reservation, since he secretly knew it was right about the correct time of year for the Hopi Indian's Snake Dance Ceremony. With the acceptance of their Indian heritage providing them with a new confidence, the siblings assumed they had an easy shoe in to be invited to attend that ceremony with the hitch hiker's family.

It would be a great honor to be invited to such a special occasion, because this is not a ceremony where white people are ever allowed to attend, and for good reason. It was, as far as Steve understood, a ceremony where numerous poisonous snakes are set loose among the dancers. He had read somewhere, that to get bitten by one of the snakes was an ordeal only those destined to be great spiritual leaders could survive.

It was likely due to this looming event that the parents of the hitch hiker weren't as welcoming to the siblings as their new found brother had promised. The mother was very distraught by their arrival, as she was sure her husband would not be happy to discover two white tourists at his home, and he was set to arrive any moment. Betz gave her the phone number, but the reassurance from her son on the other end of the phone only calmed her down slightly. She seemed tormented by their visit, even though she knew her son's heart was in the right place. She could also see that the siblings were genuine in their quest to learn about their heritage. Still, she remained concerned about how her husband would react to their presence there.

Out of respect for their recent relative and to alleviate her worries, Betz and Steve decided they should leave for a couple days and come back when her son was due home. They learned that the ceremony wasn't going to happen before then anyway, so they could just go find the campground the mother said was located just beyond the border of the reservation. What they found at that campground was so shocking that it planted a memory neither Steve nor Betz would ever forget.

The first thing they noticed upon their arrival was that some campers were leaving this very nice yet nearly empty campground. It was late afternoon, so this was not the time of day to be leaving a campground to continue a journey. By the time those campers left, the campground was completely empty, except for Betz and Steve. With their pick of camp sites, they chose the best one only a couple of sites away from the outhouse. As they were setting up their camp, Steve was the first requiring a trip to relieve himself. Betz was surprised when he came running back in a state of exhilaration as he directed her to look at the 2nd campsite over from them. When she did, she couldn't believe her eyes.

    Steve led the way, as they cautiously walked over to the campsite next to the outhouse for a closer inspection. In the center of the campsite next to the fire pit was the head of what looked like a wolf coming out of the ground with its nose pointing straight up to the sky and its mouth wide open as if howling to the night. It appeared as if the animal had been buried to its neck and then left there to die in horrendous torture. The look on its face was clearly one of an animal in great distress as it must have howled itself to death with its eyes wide open. Even with the eye balls missing, the age of the dead skin made it appear to have happened only a few days ago.

    The siblings saw this as a sign or an omen telling them they needed to leave, and it was more than either of them wanted to camp next to anyway. So, they loaded up the van and headed back across the border into the Hopi reservation. They now understood why the campground was empty, and decided the wolf must have been planted there to ward off evil spirits, namely, white tourists. It was nearly time for the Snake Dance ceremony, after all, and the last thing the Hopi people wanted was some lost tourists showing up in the middle of their sacred celebration.

    Steve and Betz, in their mind, were not lost tourists. They were invited guests with Indian ancestry surging through their veins. So, they had no intention of leaving the Hopi reservation before the Snake Dance ceremony took place. In their ignorance, they thought they could go find the grounds where the event was to take place, and locate a suitable campsite near there until their hitch hiker friend came home.

With that in mind, they stopped the van at a trading post where there were a few Indian elders sitting on some benches outside. Steve approached the elders, explained their Indian ancestry and quest to learn about their heritage, as he asked directions to the ceremonial grounds. The elders were very cordial as they described in great detail how Steve could find the way to "where they needed to go".

Feeling confident in the map he was now armed with in his mind, Steve drove for an hour before the realization hit him. Those kind and accommodating Indian elders had given Steve directions that would lead them directly out of the Hopi reservation. They had to, once again, face their whiteness and their tourist identity, and accept that they were just not welcome there. Continuing forward on the road they'd been directed to take, they soon discovered it was leading to the Grand Canyon National Park, which sounded like a good place to stop anyway.

It just so happened that their timing turned out to be the perfect time of year to hit the Grand Canyon if you were seeking a job for the summer. Even though that wasn't their intention, it sounded like a great idea once they'd arrived. For the first month or so working there, Steve couldn't see the point of living in the dorms provided for the Grand Canyon employees, since it wasn't free. Betz was open to whatever her brother wanted to do, since she was thoroughly enjoying their outdoor adventure together. So, the siblings found a good camping spot just beyond the border of the park to call home.

The day soon approached, when Steve informed Betz of the plan he had made with their older brother, Gary, to meet up and further explore their beautiful country together. This was not good news to Betz, however, because she was having the time of her life at the Grand Canyon. It was very much like the college life she'd missed out on, with the close comradery among the employees and the parties sometimes reaching well into the night.

Betz had never gotten to know her older brother anyway, since he was rarely home and only bullied her when he was around. To her, staying at the Canyon, moving into the dorms with her friends, was a much more inviting scenario. Not able to change her mind, Steve went his way to meet up with his brother, leaving Betz behind at the Grand Canyon to grow up on her own.

With her brother gone, Betz settled into herself with a life more suited to her. It included fewer parties, since she never did enjoy drinking, and closer friendships with her fellow workers. It was within days of her 19th birthday, when Betz was chosen by Spirit to have the most astounding spiritual experience of her life. Could it be, that those Hopi Indian elders knew the Grand Canyon truly was the place where Betz, at least, really did need to go, just as they had told Steve? After all, the siblings needed to land a job there while they were hiring, because the Great Spirit had something special planned for Betz on this memorable day.

She'd gotten a day off work when all her fellow work mates were scheduled to work. That was extremely rare and hit her in a privately fearful way, since it meant another forced day in solitude. She recalled a day in her early teens, when her older brother, Gary, had told her she would have to learn how to enjoy herself by herself. All of her family

The Grand Canyon

were going off in separate directions with their own holiday plans, none of which included her. Gary was the only one to notice Betz's dilemma that day, but he obviously didn't understand her, since she'd spent most of her life fundamentally by herself. Betz was hurt by the complete disregard from her family, and insulted by her brother's comments, while at the same time she knew he was right.

Armed to the gills with her favorite crafts and a book to read just in case the boredom got too great, she loaded her dog in the car and headed for the park to spend the holiday alone. She learned that day, as she watched the ducks play and the birds sing, that she could enjoy herself by herself as long as she spent her time with nature. On this day at the Grand Canyon, she decided she would do exactly that to face this day ahead of once again having to play alone.

She set out that morning to do just that, starting with a cave she'd discovered a few weeks earlier about 50-100 feet down into the walls of the Canyon. It was a bit dangerous to get to, evidenced by the wall blocking the way to the cave designed to keep tourists at a safe distance. But, the danger in getting there was part of the fun of it, and when alone with nature at her private cave she could feel at peace with Mother Earth and all its wonders.

After spending some time looking out over the serene beauty of the Canyon walls, and watching the ravens dance an airborne spectacular for their mates, Betz was ready to venture further. She climbed out of the Canyon to explore some areas of the park she hadn't yet been to. Heading towards the woods on the other side, away from the hotels and tourists, Betz was ready to take this day on.

As she walked, each step was a new discovery including her first white forest. She found herself walking among a large group of serene Aspen trees with their white bark shining back at her, making the entire area seem brighter than any other forest she'd ever seen. Within the white forest, Betz came across a small natural meadow, where a family of three deer were having a sip of water from the small creek meandering through.

As soon as her eyes fell on that breath taking scene, she stopped in her tracks not more than 20 feet away to quietly take it all in. She stood there engrossed in their natural beauty, hoping not to scare them away, when the adult female looked up at her with those big, brown, knowing eyes of hers. Obviously feeling no threat from Betz, the peaceful creature gave her a wink of understanding and tolerance as she turned back to continue sipping the spring fresh water. Betz felt honored that such beautiful animals were willing to share their white forest with her and have no fear.

That's the way her entire day went. A truly gorgeous day filled with the kind of peace and tranquility only found by sharing time with nature. It is highly likely that what happened to her next required that serene state of her consciousness for it to be possible. At the time, Betz could not fathom any reason she would be chosen to have such a profound and wondrous experience. It came as a complete and total shock to her, an experience so overwhelming, that it left her a changed person forever.

It was around 4:00 in the afternoon on this late summer day of 1972. Betz had returned to an area in front of the Bright Angel Lodge where the tourists drive the loop. She sat down on a bench there, under a tree at one end of the loop, when something really strange started happening to her. The first thing she noticed was a tremendous feeling of joy overcoming her. It was so intense that her entire

The Grand Canyon

body seemed to vibrate from the effects of this continuous rush of exhilarating joy overwhelming her consciousness.

This Joy, capitalizing it now out of respect for its purity and intensity, rapidly exceeded any pleasurable moment she'd ever experienced before. It was far more than any delightful experience possible from within the physical realm. The vibration accompanying the breathtaking Joy was felt throughout her body from head to toe. The exultation was so penetrating, that it felt like her body would literally shatter apart from the ecstatic sensations as her consciousness was being taken higher and higher. Imagine if you can, a Joy so overpowering that Betz was feeling every cell in her body vibrate heartily from the intensity of it all the way up on this crazy ride.

It was quite a long way up too, where her consciousness was being taken by some unknown force. Just when Betz became sure her body was going to burst apart from the vibration of higher and higher frequencies, her consciousness would briefly pause in its incline. It was as if whatever force was taking her on this uphill climb was purposely stopping to allow her body barely enough time to adjust to these new dimensions. Then, just as her body would catch up, the journey would resume again taking her consciousness even higher, causing the Joy to become even stronger yet, until she felt again like she was going to burst wide open from this wonderful feeling of incredibly pure Joy.

This stopping and starting an upward journey of exhilarating Joy and raising of consciousness repeated several times, until the Joy was so overwhelming, that Betz felt like crying and laughing and screaming with Joy, all at the same time. Finally, once she recovered her breath and her body caught up with where her Spirit was taking her,

Vision Of Truth

Betz realized that she had reached her destination, where she noticed immediately there was much more than Joy here.

Within the ecstatic Joy still resonating within her, she realized she was also feeling a tremendous, all encompassing, perfectly pure, unconditional, unselfish Love. There is no purer Love for all of mankind and for all that exists in the universe, than what Betz felt that day. She was so full of Love for all, and so overwhelmed with Joy, that there was no doubt in her mind, she was no longer within the normal plane of physical existence.

Betz was at a level of awareness much higher than the rest of mankind, experiencing a different dimension from life on earth. She was definitely not within the realm of physical man, but rather, she was in the spiritual world, in the realm of Spirit. And yet, everything of her physical world was still a part of her reality as she stood there next to the bench fully aware of her natural surroundings.

Following immediately after the overwhelming sensation of Love filled her consciousness, another realization came to her. This realm of Spirit delivered, as if tagging a ride on the perfect Love, an immense warehouse of knowledge. Instantly, Betz knew all there ever was to know about everything throughout the entire infinity of the cosmos and covering all the eternity of reality. Betz suddenly had the complete knowledge of every topic, and all the history, present situations and future potentials surrounding anything and everything, and it was as if she'd always already known it. She had no questions what-so-ever, because she already knew all the answers.

As she looked around at her environment with new eyes of wisdom, she noticed there was something very different about her immediate surroundings. Everywhere

The Grand Canyon

she looked the world appeared much brighter than it had just moments before. The leaves in the trees and the grass and every green forest plant around her all radiated a beautiful glimmer. Even the tree trunks and the rocks glowed much brighter than how they appeared from the physical realm, but the glimmering affect was only prevalent where any green part of nature was concerned.

The grass and leaves were literally twinkling, as if they were covered with glitter, or better yet, it was like every blade of grass and every leaf on every tree was a bright green ember of fire. Just like the coals of a fire twinkle in and out of their many shades of bright red, orange and gold, every green plant surrounding her looked like embers of fire from within the spiritual realm, except they radiated between various shades of green instead of gold.

Within the wisdom of her mind, Betz also knew what she was looking at in these glowing embers, what was causing them to glimmer, and why the world appeared so much brighter from the spiritual realm. It was a form of energy she was witnessing flow between, among, and even through and within, every single thing surrounding her, even solid rock. In this state of enlightenment, she knew, as an absolute fact, that this same energy was flowing throughout the universe, literally connecting all that exists.

What she saw, and felt, and still knows, is that we are all truly connected at the very core of our being by this energy. It's not a legend the Indians made up, it's not a fairy tale, or a bunch of empty words. It is the truth, the absolute reality of mankind and the universe, that we are all One.

As she looked upon this glorious scene of glowing embers, she also understood what this energy actually was, and why it was making everything surrounding her appear to be brighter. She knew instantly this energy, literally speaking, is Love energy, because its source and essence is Love, which she also completely understood in its entirety. She knew where it came from, what it did for humanity and for the universe, and even how human kind can access its power for the greater good. This was the universal energy of Love that she was witnessing flow throughout the entire universe, and in her mind's eye, she could even see it in the air we breathe.

Because the immense Love she was feeling for humanity was overwhelming her entire consciousness, the only topic she could explore further in this vast knowledge available to her was the human condition out of her concern for it. Immediately upon having feelings of compassion for her fellow man, she found herself looking at the planet earth with her mind's eye as if she were 1000's of miles out in space. It felt like she was actually there looking over the globe from a great distance away with her right eye, while her left eye continued to observe her current local surroundings.

Feeling empowered with this new ability to see, Betz decided to focus closer in on a single city, namely New York City, not as a personal preference, but as a place where she knew there would be a lot of people. She wanted to look closer at humanity itself, to see what was going on in their lives, to feel what they were feeling out of her compassion for them. From a viewpoint near the top of the tallest building, as if she were in a hovering helicopter near Times Square, she watched intently as those very busy people ran to and fro. It seemed as if everything was happening all at once, because she was watching from the perspective of eternal time, where there is no past or future, only present time.

The Grand Canyon

It didn't surprise Betz, when she felt the combined weight on the shoulders of every person as a whole as they worried about their particular situation in life. She knew she could have zoomed in further, on any one individual she wanted to focus on, and she would have known all there was to know about that person's past, present and future. That is how complete this all-knowingness experience was for her. But, it wasn't necessary to concentrate on anyone in particular, because everyone on the planet was facing the same turmoil of life on earth, and she Loved them all equally.

With this much knowledge at her beck and call, you would think she would jump at this chance to find out everything there was to know about her own life or future, or that of her friends and family. But, there was actually not one single thought of her life or her future or anything that personally affected her or her loved ones throughout this experience in the spiritual realm, not even for a flicker of a moment. Selfishness, in any form of the word, was completely and absolutely absent from this higher dimension, even though this was not a brief experience for Betz.

She was in that state of all-knowing wisdom, unconditional Love and overwhelming Joy for the rest of the day, and to a lesser degree, well into the next day. And yet, it never even occurred to her to bring to mind the answers about anything personal, or for that matter, about anything she'd ever wondered about spiritually or otherwise. There was nothing to wonder about, after all, since she knew all the answers, and they were the same for everyone.

Besides, she Loved everyone in the world much greater than she had ever loved any one person in her life, so people she knew personally were equally as precious as all the people of the planet in her current state of mind. More importantly, from the revelations of the immense knowledge, she could clearly see what truly matters in all our lives, making all those things she had wondered about before this experience trivial by comparison.

Without even contemplating on any topic, she knew all about life, and the purpose of mankind and of life itself, and what everything is for, and what really matters, and what doesn't matter at all. The one thing that held the first and foremost position of importance above all she now knew, was that LOVE IS ALL THAT MATTERS. Another thing she could clearly see, as if it were the easiest thing to grasp in the world, was that the problems of mankind would literally disappear from their lives if they could only Love all that is.

She saw all the people of the planet struggling within the tremendous trivia that defined their daily lives, and she knew they were missing the point of it all. She knew how they could escape from all their problems. The answer to their freedom from strife was so simple and obvious, from within that realm of knowledge, that she was shocked she hadn't realized the way out of the struggles of life long before this.

There Betz stood, next to her little bench in the Grand Canyon drive loop, completely astonished by all these tremendous revelations going on in her mind. This was some very important information that she was being privy to. She needed to tell people. She wanted to shout it out to the world right there and then. She knew the answer to all the problems facing mankind! What an incredible gift!

With this gift came a tremendous responsibility, however, equaled only by the Joy and Love she was feeling. She absolutely had to share her Love and this news with people. The need to share felt so strong within her, that she simply HAD to share it with somebody, with anybody, right there and then.

In an attempt to satisfy her need to share her revelations and express her overwhelming Love for her fellow man, she went inside the Bright Angel Lodge, the closest location where she knew she would find people. There were 5 people standing around the fireplace in the lobby after just having returned from a hike down into the Canyon. She stood among them with a huge smile on her face, since the Joy still remaining within her simply could not be contained or hidden.

Listening to them revisit their adventure and to their laughter as they reviewed various highlights of their climb, she waited patiently, as they chatted on and on about their special journey. Finally, the man standing next to Betz turned and looked at her. She leaped at the opportunity to share her Joy and Love. She threw her arms around his neck and whispered in his ear, "I Love you".

WHOOPS!! Wait a minute!! Did she really do that? What could this poor man be thinking! Well, this was definitely not going to work! She suddenly knew, as a part of the wisdom within her, that there was no point in speaking. Immediately upon telling that man of her Love for him, she realized it was impossible for her to speak at all from the spiritual realm and have anyone from the physical dimension understand her words. As soon as she made the attempt, she knew absolutely, she could not communicate from this higher plane!

Her body seemed to respond just fine to walking, and she could see, hear and smell just like always, but something wasn't quite right when it came to speaking. She had no idea what that man actually heard her say, since her own ears only heard her tell him that she Loved him. But she knew as fact, by way of the all-knowingness she still maintained, that it did her no good to speak, since nobody could understand a word she was saying. So, without even waiting for a reaction from the man she was hugging, she turned and ran from the Lodge and went back to her bench where this all began.

Betz now realized she was faced with a serious dilemma. Here she was, vibrating on another plane, in another dimension from everyone else. Within that dimension, she could see things, she knew things, revelations that are important for the rest of the world to know. And yet, she couldn't, from this higher plane, share this information with the rest of the population. This new realization saddened her greatly. Betz felt tremendous compassion for the people of the world and for all the problems they carry around, when they don't have to.

There she stood, with the answers to all their life struggles and goals, with the key to true and everlasting happiness for all, and she couldn't do anything to help them from where she stood in this higher vibration, because she couldn't even begin to communicate with the lower physical plane. All Betz wanted to do was help the population of the world escape the hold their physical struggles have over them. She wanted to share this knowledge so they could know how to be truly free. And yet, from where she stood, she was completely helpless to them.

She knew what she had to do. As much as she hated to leave the spiritual realm of ecstatic Joy and Love, she had to come back down to the lower physical dimension with the rest of the world. She simply had to share this information with her fellow man. The feeling of

The Grand Canyon

responsibility to help humanity was so strong, that there was simply no choice to be made in her mind. Like when your house catches on fire and you risk your life to save your children from dying in the fire. You have the choice of just running for your own life, and letting your children die, but it's not even an option you recognize as a choice.

The responsibility to help humanity was so important to Betz, that the choice was that obvious. She simply must share this life altering new information with the rest of the world. For her to communicate this to people, however, she would have to return to their level. She realized her ability to speak in their language wasn't the only problem. In order to know how to deliver this knowledge to them, she would have to experience their troubles right along with them. Unless she was at the level where she could share in their sorrows, she would never be able to describe to them how to make the sorrows go away.

The thought of leaving the ecstatic Joy of her experience behind saddened Betz further, but just as instantly as she had that concern, she knew absolutely that she would return to experience that highest spiritual realm again someday, once she'd fulfilled her reason for returning to the physical plane of existence. With that realization, she also knew she would be able to bring others back with her so they could share the experience together, which gave her some relief from the regret of leaving this beautiful realm behind.

After all, the only missing component from the wondrous experience she was having, which would have made it absolute perfection, was having someone there to share it with her, someone she could hug who would hug her back with equal enthusiasm. She longed so greatly to share the overwhelming Love she had for everyone with someone, to throw her arms around an actual person who she knew could understand the depth of her Loving gesture towards them. She was grateful to know she would be able to return to this realm of euphoria and bring someone, perhaps even many, to share it with her someday.

As soon as the decision was made, to take on the responsibility of sharing this new information with humanity, she felt a very slight shift in her body, as if she was no longer being held in position by some unseen force. It was as if she was now free to leave, if that was to be her choice, but the choice was still up to her, and there would have been no judgment of her regarding what choice she would have made. That's when she first recognized she actually did have the option of staying in this state of utopia forever if she wanted to, since prior to that she'd only seen her return to help humanity as the only responsible direction to take rather than a choice she was making.

Even though choosing to stay would have resulted in her physical death eventually, since even the selfishness of survival was meaningless trivia from the spiritual perspective, it carried no weight in her decision to return to fulfill her spiritual promise. The only thing that mattered to her was to help the humanity she Loved so completely escape from the prison they made for themselves. Betz was content with the choice she'd made. She knew the first step in fulfilling that duty was to get herself back down to the assumed reality of the physical world.

With the slight shift in her body, she began focusing on returning to the physical realm. She quickly realized that going back down to the physical dimension was not going to be an effort free journey like the trip up to the spiritual realm had been. It was not a round trip taxi ride. She had to make a strong conscious and consistent effort to bring

The Grand Canyon

herself down from that higher level of vibration. In fact, it was a long and difficult process that took several hours, well into the next day, and even, to some degree, the day after that. It was a very slow decent, a concerted effort with very little sleep, if any, during the journey.

With her consciousness so far removed from the physical world she was trying to return to, she felt her best bet would be to return to her dorm room where she could be alone to concentrate on the decline. As long as she remained surrounded by the beauty of the glowing embers of green leaves everywhere, it remained difficult to pursue the darker road. She began the long walk back to the dorm buildings enjoying every step along the way as she continued to marvel at the beauty of the world from her new perspective.

She knew she still couldn't communicate, and wanted to try to avoid bumping into anyone who might know her. So, she purposely chose to take the rarely used side entry into the dorm building. Unfortunately, she wasn't successful in avoiding a chance meeting with a good friend in the hallway to her room. He blocked her path as he greeted her with excitement informing her of a small gathering they were putting together in one of their work mate's rooms.

This put Betz in a bad situation, since even if she could speak in a language he and their friends could understand, she would only want to talk about a Love way too immense for them to comprehend. She was not currently the same person her friend was inviting to a get together. She had to try to respond to her friend, but with her thoughts so clouded by Love, she didn't know what to say or how to say it. The words that came out were as jumbled in her mind as they must have sounded coming out of her mouth.

She knew immediately, again, there was simply no point in trying to communicate. She looked at him speaking with Love in her heart and words, knowing he only heard garbled noises, longing for his sake to be back to normal enough for him to be able to hear her. He looked back at her completely puzzled, even cocking his head to one side in his confusion. She knew there was no hope in resolving this communication issue. All she could do is shake her head as she turned to leave him behind in his bewilderment.

The next day, Betz was still very high from the experience of the day before, when the same male friend from the night before approached her to ask what was wrong with her when they last met. She knew she could finally communicate, but had no answers to his question. How could she possibly explain what had happened to her? All she could do is tell him she'd had a spiritual experience, and was still having it, as she got up and walked away from him once again.

Betz would forever be changed by this experience, as she remained very conscious of the duty she came back the physical realm to fulfill. She maintained a complete memory of all the knowledge she learned that day and her Love for humanity also remained strong. Even though it was tempered substantially by the physical attributes of the world, she remembered the intensity of the Love she felt and continued in her conviction to help her beloved brethren discover that depth of meaning in their lives.

She also knew instinctively, however, that the world wasn't ready for what she had to say. She had no choice but to just get on with her life, with the understanding that

The Grand Canyon

she would know what to do with all that information she was shown, when it was time for her to disclose it to the world. All she could do in the meantime is put it behind her and wait for that time to come.

My Travels

That day has finally come. This is a true story, and my nickname is Betz. It's been over 42 years since the astounding true experience I just described actually happened to me. It is with this series of books that I am hoping to finally fulfill that responsibility to share the information I was shown with the world. There is much to tell, more than can fit in any one book, but before I can even start I have to first tell you my story. To send home the weight and importance of the news I have to say, it will be helpful for you to know what brought me to this day.

This isn't just some air head author who had a freaky experience one day and now thinks they know how to solve all your problems. My life has been filled by one profound spiritual experience after another forcing me to never forget or get distracted from the importance of fulfilling my spiritual obligation. I live only to teach others the many spiritual truths I've been shown, along with some proofs, that they are the absolute realities of mankind. One of those proofs is my spiritual life story.

I started out this spiritual memoir with my Grand Canyon experience mostly because it was the first major experience in my life, but it actually started when I was a very young child of about 7 years old. To sum up those childhood years, I was clearly informed through a series of numerous dreams, that I have a "predestiny". I spent years pondering whether I even believed in predestiny, and have come to realize, for those of you who don't believe in it either, that our free will always takes precedence.

The best way to look at predestiny is as more of a predisposition, not something ground in stone. It's what we come into this life to achieve, but our free will can alter that predisposed life plan at any or every step along the way. Yes, I was predestined to do this and more, but I always had the choice of following it through or throwing it away and doing my own thing. It's not that we are robots following a pre-drawn map, but to help us on our educational journey of life, our soul does have a plan for us before we are ever born.

After all that has happened to me, I've come to realize that I am here for a very specific reason, a purpose that is too important for Spirit to allow my free will to throw it away, since every time I've tried my life turns into a devastating mess. The new information I'm here to share with the world is too important to be left up to humanity to figure out on their own, since left to their own perceptions, there is a very good chance they will never put it together. It is simply too obvious for the complex human mind to grasp, especially when we are coming from a place of darkness in a state of total amnesia, completely unaware of our own divinity. To illustrate why I say this is what makes telling my spiritual story a crucial part of the evidence humanity will need to see the truth of my words.

The Journey Continues

To resume my story from that Grand Canyon experience, my brothers did return to the Canyon to retrieve me, but I was a changed person, and refused to leave with them once again. There was still some time left in the fall to continue to work at the Grand Canyon, which I did well into November and was one of the last temporary employees to leave. I'd met some people who were about to travel east, and upon promising them a Floridian escape from the coming winter cold, they were happy to make room for me. Along that journey, they became fast friends who I traveled and lived with for a couple years beyond that first meeting.

After traveling to my home town in Florida to visit my Mom, where, as usual, my friends were not welcome, we all moved to the town where my Dad had a new rental business with an apartment above his shop. We lived there for the entire winter, enjoying the Florida weather and earning some travel money. It was a good season, but the day came when it was time to move on.

My boyfriend, whom I'd met only a couple months prior, was getting ready to go home to Michigan, where he was the lead in a rock 'n roll band. I was ready to hit the road as well. My Grand Canyon friends and I wanted to return to the Canyon and perhaps work there another summer, so we were planning to travel west again. I felt very close to this boyfriend, so losing him was a sad situation for me, but I was just not willing to follow him around like a groupie. Besides, he never invited me.

My Sweet Angel

It was the day before we headed out for Arizona with the initial plan to visit my brother, Steve, who now lived in Tucson, when my next spiritual experience took place. It was about 7 months following my Grand Canyon experience, early in April of the next year. Since my boyfriend and I were going in different directions, I was feeling especially melancholy that day.

Ever since my connection with Mother Earth at the Grand Canyon, I would always seek out special locations near home where I could commune with nature whenever I felt the need. Well, I felt the need this day due to the inevitable love loss I was facing. So, I took a walk by myself down to my favorite spot by the lake and sat on my bench, the only bench there.

Feeling particularly gloomy, I said out loud, since I was completely alone, "There is no such thing as happiness, it's just a stupid word". That's right, folks. The same person who experienced the ultimate height of joy in the truest sense of the word only a half a year ago was squarely back in the real world of feeling sorry for herself.

Suddenly, out of nowhere, I heard the words in a gentle female voice, "You will not be happy as long as you are here." Whoa!! What was that! I looked around to see if there was someone hiding behind a tree somewhere, but I was entirely alone. Besides, it was a clear voice I was hearing, as if a young woman were standing right in front of me.

Okay..., this is awesome. I wondered what would happen if I responded to this beautiful voice. Never expecting, but only hoping, to hear from her again, I said, "What should I do, where should I go?" Sure enough, to my delight and surprise, there was a response. She said again, as gently as the breeze, "You will not be happy as long as you are here." Then she added, "That is all I can tell you now."

Wow!! This is really happening! I am talking with an angel! This was soooo cool, I thought, anxious to hold on to this experience as long as possible. I wanted to keep

My Travels

the conversation going, so I said, "How long will I have to wait?" I knew she had just told me she couldn't tell me anymore, so again, I didn't expect a response. I just figured it was worth a try. I was so excited when she did respond again. It was as if she was waiting for me to ask the right question, one she could answer.

In that gentle voice of hers, she responded with words I will never forget, "It will be 20-25 years". Then she repeatedly stated the same words she'd started this conversation with as her voice faded away, "You will not be happy as long as you are here, you will not be happy as long as you are here..." And she was gone.

As soon as I knew it was over, I started crying out loud! I not only cried, I bawled! I was bawling because I was going to have to wait 20-25 years before I would be happy. How dreadful! Then, suddenly the tears stopped as quickly as they came. I stopped crying because I suddenly realized, there was hope. I now knew, beyond any shadow of a doubt, that someday I would be happy. What a precious gift that was.

Did you notice something strange about that message from the angel? For one thing, she didn't seem to know exactly when I finally would be happy. She said it would be 20-25 years. There's a 5 year period that was up for grabs. You'd think an angel would know exactly when my life would be happy. And there was that other confusing part in her message as well. Where was "here"?

I was getting ready to leave Florida, but I knew instinctively it wasn't Florida she was talking about. In fact, I traveled all over the country for years and always knew in my heart that none of those places were the "here" she was talking about. I never could figure out what "here" might mean. I just knew, that when it was time for me to know, I would know, just like the Grand Canyon experience. It was all just too much to wrap my brain around, so I just metaphorically shook my head in bewilderment and went on with life.

Well, that was it. I was left on my own from the point when the angel left me to fend for myself for the next 20 years. No more wondrous messages or spiritual experiences. Even though the wait was long, I was always thankful for my sweet angel's message. It brought me hope every time I thought I was out of hope through those 20 years of turmoil in my life. I was still very lacking in anything religious, never went to church, never even read books on spirituality or any other subject. I never have been much of a reader (much less a writer).

I continued to try to connect to nature whenever possible, my only resource for anything uplifting. Mostly, I just muddled along like the rest of us, even losing sight of any purpose in life. One thing I knew, from both of those experiences, is that I had some sorrows to go through. I knew the time for me to understand why I had those wonderful experiences would come, and then I would also know what I was supposed to do about it. So, I left it at that, and never really tried to figure it all out.

A Vietnam Veteran's Parade

It was nearly 20 years later, when my husband and I were living in Seattle under very poor conditions. We had just gone bankrupt due to an accident at my husband's work. It took my husband's thumb off causing him to be out of work for 9 months straight as he was recovering from corrective surgery. The profession my husband was in, a diesel mechanic, required full use of his thumb, since he couldn't even turn a bolt without it.

My husband was not the type of person to pursue assistance from the government, however, so when he got injured, he never even tried to get compensation from welfare or workman's comp for his injury. He accepted their free medical assistance, but beyond that, we never even filed for food stamps. We just survived off our credit cards until it became an insurmountable debt, and then just gave up altogether when they came to repossess the house we owned in Montana at the time.

We both had jobs by now, after finally moving to Seattle to find them, but we were way too far in debt to maintain both rent and a mortgage, especially once our lawyer tenant took advantage of us from all those miles away. I'll never do business with a lawyer again, but that's another story and not a spiritual one.

It was shortly after our bankruptcy, while still living in very poor conditions, when another spiritual experience happened. This time it was my husband who was chosen for this wondrous encounter, but I'm including it here, because it directly affected us both in a very big way.

We'd received a very surprising invitation in the mail the day before it happened. It was from Australia, of all places, where the Australian military was inviting my husband and I to come to their country to join in on their "Welcome Home Vietnam Veteran's Parade" and homecoming celebration. What most people don't realize is the Australians fought side by side with the Americans in the Vietnam War, and Larry even knew some of them as comrades when he was there.

In looking back on this all these years later, there is one thing worth pointing out. What made this invitation so extremely bizarre is the question it brings to mind. How in the world did they find us at our very recent meek abode?

We'd only lived there less than a month, and had moved several times during the short year or so we'd lived in Seattle, starting out the first 3 months living in a travel trailer at a campground. It's not like our address could have been internationally updated every few weeks.

Realize; this was long before the internet held any worthwhile information, since it didn't even exist yet then. I remember the old "bulletin boards" being used in those days, the predecessor to the internet. So, how that invitation found its way to us goes way beyond the imagination. I'm pointing this out, because it's worth recognizing how Spirit works. When something is meant to be put in your path to lead you to your destiny, nothing will block its way. Trying to figure out the odds of how it could be possible is simply a waste of time.

My husband was very upset over the invitation, because he so badly wanted to go, but there was no way we could afford it. Since it was over $800 per plane ticket just to get there, which was a lot of money back then, we really had no hope of being able to go. My husband was so disappointed. I've never seen him want anything so badly. I was sorry for him, and hated having to be the realistic voice.

The next day, as he often enjoyed doing, he was taking our dog on a long walk in a large overgrown field not far from the small house we were renting. When he came back, he had something very important he wanted to talk to me about, something he didn't know how to process on his own. He knew I made it a practice to pay attention to the messages animals might bring us, which was part of my Indian heritage I'd always been intrigued by. He sat me down and proceeded to tell me his story.

He and our German Shepard mix had only been walking about 4 or 5 minutes when a falcon came and sat on a branch right in front of him on the path. He said the bird was right at eye level, and it looked straight at him. The astounding sight stopped him in his tracks, as the dog kept running ahead down the path. He said he just stood there staring at the majestic bird for a minute or so, which he said couldn't have been more than a few feet in front of him, when the dog came running back to find him. With the dog's sudden appearance, the falcon flew away, leaving him to marvel over that wondrous experience, expecting it to be over. It wasn't over.

The bird came back a few yards down the path, and again landed on a branch directly in front of him staring him straight in the face once again. As he stood there enchanted by this magnificent encounter, a few minutes went by before the dog came looking for him again. What really fascinated me, as I sat there listening to this story, is that the bird wasn't scared away by the dog this time. Larry and this beautiful bird just remained eye locked as the dog came bounding up to them like a reckless sailor.

Realizing Larry wasn't giving the dog the attention he expected, the dog followed Larry's glance and finally noticed the bird. Being a dog, as dogs tend to be, he decided to be the tough protector and went after the bird with a sudden vengeance, barking like an idiot. Larry stopped the dog, but was disappointed that it wasn't enough, since the dog did manage to scare the bird away. Again, Larry thought it was over, and was disappointed that the dog had spoiled it for him. But yet again, this magnificent falcon still wasn't done with my husband that day.

Vision Of Truth

On the third visit, everything happened as before, except the falcon stood its ground this time, or should I say, its branch. As before, the dog spotted the bird and again began to step up to ruin the moment by chasing the bird away. But, Larry managed to stop the dog this time, before it started barking or jumping after the bird. Being very close to Larry, I imagine the dog understood Larry was very intrigued by this bird, so he just sat down and stared at the bird right along with Larry.

The amazing thing to me, is even with all this going on, the bird didn't fly away this time, even with the dog sitting right there staring at it. It wasn't long before the dog got bored with the staring game and went his merry way down the path leaving Larry and the falcon behind. Larry told me, that he and the bird continued to stare at each other for quite a while. He said he began to talk softly to the bird, asking what it was trying to tell him. He said this went on for what seemed like 10 amazing minutes, when the bird finally flew away on its own merits and the experience was over.

Now, I've seen a lot of animals delivering messages, sometimes called omens, but nothing ever so intense as this, not even close. It usually is a bird that does deliver messages, but the hawk is normally the message carrier. I've never heard of a falcon showing up at all in any omen ever, since they are such a rare bird anyway. Owls are always bad news, according to most Indian beliefs, but I had no idea what the falcon represented. So, without that knowledge to fall back on, I thought we should look at it another way.

The thing I have learned over the many years of watching for omens and messages from animals, ever since that Indian hitch hiker taught me about omens, is to pay attention to what you are doing or thinking about just before the message is delivered. If you are driving, for example, and a hawk shows up in a particular way, then you should slow down and pay close attention to what's happening on the road. This has actually saved me from both traffic accidents and traffic tickets on several occasions.

But, this was very different in some important ways. The falcon wasn't flying any sort of pattern, for one thing, and it was a very rare bird doing something falcons just don't do. Plus, it was looking right at him, letting me know it was a direct message for him, not a warning or an omen of any kind, but a specific message.

As I think about this now, there is something else I just realized about this experience. The fact that the bird came back 3 times means this was a very spiritual experience, and therefore, a spiritual message. There is something very powerful in that number 3. Everything seems to come to me in sets of three. Watch for it in the spiritual stories to come.

My husband really needed some answers right then, so there was no time to do any research into the Indian teachings of what meaning a falcon may carry. Besides, this was so far outside of the norm; I didn't think any research would come close to the weight this experience carried. So, I fell back on what I'd learned by my own experience over the years.

I asked my husband, "What were you thinking about at the time, as you were walking down the path before the bird first arrived?" He said he was thinking about that Australian invitation, and wondering how he could find the money to go. As soon as he said that, I knew right away what the bird was trying to tell him.

Surprised and delighted by what I had to say, I told him straight out, "Well then, pack your bags darling, because we're going to Australia!!" He looked at me in shock, "are you sure?" Absolutely, I was sure, because you just don't have something like that happen to you without a serious message being behind it all. That bird was telling Larry that the money would come, and boy, did it ever.

Over the next few weeks, money seemed to fall out of the trees above us. People came forward who owed us money we'd forgotten about. Refunds from deposits on utility companies showed up in the mail. I even remember getting a substantial check as payment for luggage an airline had lost way back when we were on our honeymoon, something like 7 years earlier. How they found us is also way beyond me, but I'm telling you, the money came in leaps and bounds without any effort on our part.

Within weeks, we had $5000 in hand, enough to take a wonderful 3 week vacation backpacking all over Australia, the best vacation we ever had in our lives. My husband proudly marched in that Vietnam Veterans Parade, with a face that beamed in pride for his accomplishments over 3 terms as a combat medic. We were among the very few Americans who made it to that Australian Vietnam Homecoming Celebration, since of course, most American Vets never got an invitation.

As I'm writing you this story, which I've told people numerous times, the tears are flowing like never before. Because, this experience not only made my dearly departed husband incredibly happy, but it was a major turning point in both of our lives. It was much more than just a wonderful vacation; it was the beginning of the rest of our lives. Because, for one thing, my husband found people there whom he'd gone to war with.

They were American expatriates who had served in his unit, which is a bond between men that never dies. We now had our best friends in the world, since I also got along really well with their wives, on the other side of the world. We hated facing our return to America, but before we ever left Australia, we decided we were going to try to see if we could move there permanently. It would require being accepted by the government of Australia, which was an unknown, but we were determined to give it our best effort.

It took us nearly 2 years to accomplish the task of processing paperwork and being welcomed to move to that beautiful country by the Australian Government, but sure enough, that day came and we were accepted. During all those efforts of preparing for our major move, never really knowing for sure whether we would be allowed to move to their country, the thought never even occurred to me.

Not until about a month before we were to actually board a plane, did I even think of my angel. It was on the day that we had finally gotten notice that we had been accepted. That's when it hit me like a ton of bricks, the "here" the angel spoke of, of course, the "here" was America!!! She told me I wouldn't be happy as long as I was in America!!

Australia Bound

Now, don't get me wrong. I love America, and have always been very patriotic, which is why this thought never even crossed my mind in all those years. It is just that I finally knew in my heart, this was it. This is what the angel meant by the word, "here". On March 31, 1990, we boarded the plane that would take us to our new home on the other side of the world.

Vision Of Truth

I wasn't exactly sure, at the time, of how long it had been since the angel had spoken to me (even though I have been able to research it for this book). I just knew it was somewhere close to 20 years. In my mind, I was on my way to, not only a whole new and exciting life in a foreign country, but I was finally going to be happy, just as I was promised by my angel! How exciting is that!

Well, it didn't go as great as I had hoped right away. The angel was right, but it hadn't been the minimum of 20 years at this point yet. I was pursuing my career as a computer programmer and basic overall settling in. There were some serious adjustments required to living in this new country, since there are a lot of differences in Australia when compared to America.

The thing to remember is Australia was founded by prisoners, who were, for the most part, "petty thieves". This affects an attitude within their society that would be unacceptable to most Americans. After living there for 8 years in total, I'll even go so far as to say, that petty theft is actually a part of the Australian economy. You either flourished in the give and take of it, therefore maintaining a "fair" way of life, or you wilted within it, as we did.

Early on, I noticed that there weren't many churches to speak of in Australia. There were a few, but no more than a third of what we have here in America, if that many, depending on what part of America. At first, I thought this lack of churches also reflected as a lack of morals, justifying the theft situation in my mind. But I was wrong. In fact, Australia is very spiritual, by far more spiritual than America. They just aren't extremely religious.

That's when I started to consciously recognize that religion and spirituality were not necessarily one in the same thing. I also now realize why I had to leave America

My Travels

to be happy. It was so I could wake up to myself, to my own Spirit. America was just not there for me spiritually. I already knew that the churches, with all their doctrines of fear, were not for me. And, with so much of that same consciousness here in America, I needed to go where the awareness of Spirit went far beyond the church walls.

To get back to my story, I was running my own computer software business by the end of 1992. I still wasn't having a good time of it, and was nowhere near anything close to happiness. However, I was warming up a bit to this new spirituality I was discovering in this new country. Although, at this point in time, I wasn't awake to myself enough to have any real questions, only curiosity. That is, until, my next spiritual experience took place.

Even though I didn't think about it at the time, through some newspaper articles that I kept, I have been able to pinpoint within days when this next major experience took place, my wake up call. It was a couple months after an article came out that I kept, which is dated Feb 13, 1993, placing it in April, 1993. I can also now pinpoint when the angel came to me as being on April 8, 1973, through a log of the journey we took immediately afterwards. As you can see, these dates are precisely 20 years apart!

Wake Up Call

It started when one of my employees for my computer software company told me of a small psychic fair she had heard about on the radio. It would be my first psychic event, and I thought it sounded like fun, so we decided to go together. Australia's psychic fairs can get as large as some county fairs are here in America. At this event, however, there were only about 8-10 "readers" and no vendors or any special speakers, nothing else. Once in a while one of the readers would give a short speech on the stage of this very small high school auditorium, where it was held. That was it.

We paid a mere $5.00, and in exchange, we could get three 15 minute readings from any of the readers we chose, which was very reasonable and sounded like fun. As soon as we went in, I saw a reader that I knew I just "had" to see. It was a man who was reading Indian Medicine Cards. Assuming it was because of my Indian heritage that I felt so immediately drawn to him, I went to the back of the very long line to see him. Growing impatient with the long wait, I went to a speech taking place on the stage, and then, since his line was still long, I went to another lady who read a ring I was wearing.

She told me I would be successful at achieving what I am meant to achieve within this lifetime, but she didn't think it related to my business or money in general. Also, she said that I had to get beyond some childhood fears that were holding me back. And finally, she said, that she was getting a very strong message for me to "go for it".

Well, that was fun, but nothing revolutionary. I was actually disappointed to hear that my business wasn't going to turn some corner and make me richer than my wildest dreams. You know, the kind of thing we all hope the future has in store for us. In other words, I was definitely not taking any of this stuff very seriously.

When she was done, and I got up from the chair, I realized that the other readers were beginning to pack up, and the place was about to close. I looked over at the Indian Medicine cards guy, and he was packing up his table with nobody waiting in line. I ran over to him and literally begged him to do one last reading for me. He gave in and sat down to do what he figured would be a super quick reading to get rid of me. However, Spirit had something else in mind for him and for me at that particular point in time.

Now first, I should describe this man to you. He was tall and thin with blonde hair and blue eyes and a very fair, light complexion on his slim, oval face. You'll understand why that is important in a minute. Anyway, I sat down, he shuffled the cards, and I cut them. Then he laid down 3 cards as I watched.

I was surprised that he was startled by the cards that came down. It was when I looked up at him, due to his gasp of alarm, that I noticed something strange was beginning to occur. At first, I didn't realize that I was having a "vision", one I learned later is called a "transmutation" (I think). It all seemed so real, as I just sat there in shock watching everything change before my eyes.

First, the room grew dark around us, as if there was a spotlight only on us as the rest of the room fell into darkness. As I looked at this man's face in response to his gasp of surprise, I noticed the corner of his jaw was moving! That's right, it was like his bones were moving under his skin!! It was a jerking motion on the lower corner of his face, as if a critter was in there trying to get out. Then his jaw just popped out from the place on his face where it belonged.

I watched mesmerized as it formed a whole new squared off shape to his jaw, but only on the one side of his face, at first. Then the other side also started to change, only this time it went a lot quicker, like it was easier the 2nd time around. Now he had a square shape to his face instead of an oval shape making it seem wider than it had been, as well.

After that the rest of his face changed much more rapidly, and all at once. His skin darkened substantially, his eyes became brown instead of blue and even his hair became black and long instead of short and blonde. Virtually every feature of this man changed to its opposite. It was like some of the special affects you see in the movies these days.

Well, I was in total shock by now, sitting there with my mouth wide open. I shook my head in bewilderment, and looked down at the cards to try to return to my normal senses. I looked up at him again in hopes all would be back to normal, but it wasn't. He was still there, plain as day, a changed man. That's when I realized that this man had transformed from a fair skinned white man to a darker skinned American Indian!!

Whoa...what does this mean? Clearly, this was another beautiful gift coming from Spirit. I knew absolutely, whatever this man had to say to me from reading these cards, I had better be listening to. This was obviously very important information I was about to be given, again. I was ready to start taking this spiritual stuff seriously.

I quickly moved my attention to what he was saying. I was actually worried that I'd been so absorbed in the vision of the transformation that I was missing the message from the cards. I was surprised to discover he had hardly said anything since my attention got distracted. It was as if time had stood still throughout that entire transformation process. It felt to me like at least a couple minutes had gone by, when according to the flow of his words, it couldn't have been more than a second, if that.

He was still in the process of telling me why he was surprised by the cards that were laid down. He said that he had been reading cards for over 10 years, and this combination of cards, especially 2 of the cards, had only come together 2 other times in all those years, I was the

My Travels

third. He said this was very significant and extremely important information for me to understand and listen to. Well, unknown to him (it seemed), I already knew that. He definitely had my complete attention!

For those of you familiar with these "Medicine" cards, the first card was the Whale, and the one right next to it was the Dolphin card. The third card, which was of lesser significance to the importance, was the Butterfly card. Well, I now own these cards myself, and even after reading what the author has to say about these particular cards repeatedly, I still got more from his actual reading than from the cards themselves.

That's the way it is with a good reading from a true psychic. Their gift is their intuition, and the cards are only a tool they use to inspire their intuition. It's their message that holds the information you are meant to hear, and the cards without the psychic are like a wagon without the horse to pull it where it's meant to go.

His reading began with the Whale, as he told me it is the holder of wisdom over all the generations of mankind. He continued to the next card, telling me that the Dolphin was the means of bringing the Whale's wisdom to fruition. He said, first of all, this means I have lived for many lifetimes, and I carry with me the memories and wisdom of all of those lifetimes. He said the Dolphin, being with the Whale, was very significant. It meant that I would be able to complete, within this lifetime, that which I have been trying to achieve all of my lifetimes before. He said I was going to finally succeed in this life, but again, it was not about the type of success money brings.

He went on to say, that the Butterfly was the card of "transformation", meaning I still had some issues to get over before I would be ready to go forward with this work.

Realizing that this information was becoming parallel to what the woman reader had just said, I asked about the butterfly card. Part of me wanted to test him as I am always moved to do, but I mostly wanted to try to pinpoint what type of issues I needed to get over. His answer was that they were fears, probably childhood fears, which again coincided with the prior reading. He said, that I would get past them soon enough, and would be ready to get on with the work I needed to do in this lifetime.

Then he said something that passed my little test well and true, not only for his reading, but also the woman's reading before him. He said that he was getting something really strong from the Dolphin, which he felt was highly unusual. He said, he was getting a message from the Dolphin, basic as they may seem, "go fishing". I looked at him confused, which moved him to clarify it further.

Without my mentioning the woman reader at all, he said, "the Dolphin is telling you to GO FOR IT"! Using the exact words the woman had just said, he repeated that I should "go for it". I said, not having a clue of what I was talking about, "I will", and he responded, "I know you will".

Then the scene changed very quickly back to normal. He no longer appeared as an Indian to me, and the lights in the room seemed to come back on. Suddenly, he threw the cards down on the table, jumped up, and almost ran away from me into the next room where the other readers were gathering to wind down from the day. I just sat there, still in shock from it all. I wanted to run over to him and ask him what had just happened. But, I couldn't even get him to glance in my direction.

It didn't matter anyway. It was an experience designed to send a very important message directly to me. He wouldn't have been able to shed any further light on it than that. At the time, however, I couldn't figure out what the message meant, starting with what I could have been trying to accomplish through all of these lives of mine. In fact, even the concept of having more than one life was pretty new to me at the time.

Reincarnation
This idea of people living many lives is probably something we should discuss before moving past this. There are a lot of people who have a problem with this belief, and many more who don't know what they think about this topic. Let's start out with some consideration on a series of questions.

How did we manage to evolve as a human species if we each started from scratch at the moment of birth? Look around, we are evolving. How is that possible in the scenario of everyone only living one life and starting out with a blank slate of consciousness? Furthermore, where do prodigies come from and geniuses? Where did all those amazing young children learn how to play the piano so well or paint the masterpiece?

For that matter, why does one new born child have a different personality from any other? If we were born with a blank slate, why does one baby cry a lot, another one act very fidgety, and yet another is born with a very calm demeanor? Our personality is a compilation of our many experiences processed by whatever our level of consciousness may be. So, if we are all starting with an empty slate of experiences and a brand new consciousness, why are we not all exactly the same from our date of birth?

The point is; how do we answer these questions and more? People prefer to not dive into these types of questions too deeply, and simply assign the blame for personality characteristics onto the parents or family interactions of the young child growing up. But, that wasn't the question. What about the new born child, the personality that happens before any parent or family members have the opportunity to change it?

There is only one answer that truly makes sense. Of course, we have to reincarnate to evolve and we must have lived a prior life to be born with a unique personality and/or talent in this life. There is simply no other answer and nothing else makes sense. The easier question is; why do so many people still fight this obvious resolution of reincarnation? Even though most religions do believe in reincarnation in one way or another, the Christian religion has a good reason for not supporting this scenario, since it would conflict with other parts of their doctrine.

I know there are going to be people who want to stay firm in their belief, that we only live this one life, and that's actually fine with me. That is, as long as those same people realize, that it doesn't require their belief for it to be true. That's simply the way it is with truth, it doesn't require anyone's awareness of it to be the reality of our existence. The world never was flat even with the entire human race believing it was.

Believe it or not, though, there is some science backing up the concept of reincarnation. There has been some serious study done on this topic, and their findings are very eye opening. There are very dedicated people working for the University of Virginia who did a major study on reincarnation that went on for 40 - 50 years. Throughout those 4-5 decades (depending on which article you read or which person you are talking about), they studied 2500 - 3000 cases of possible reincarnation claims, where very young children would tell their parents of facts from their prior life.

My Travels

For more information on these people and their work, you can visit their websites included in the references section at the back of this book. The links will take you to a discussion on Dr. Ian Stevenson's life work and to an article written by Jim B. Tucker, an associate psychiatry professor at the University of Virginia Medical Center's Division of Perceptual Studies. They have both written books on their findings as well, and there are many other avenues of research on this subject if you care to pursue it further.

What we are talking about is a study of very young toddlers, starting at the age of 2 years old, telling their parents who they ARE, which conflicted with who their parents were telling them they now were. As they struggled adjusting to this new life they were finding themselves in, insisting they were someone else, the parents would grow concerned, which is how these cases came to be. What we need to realize, is these very young children gave actual historic facts that could be researched and found to be accurate.

One such case, for example, told his Christian parents his full name, the name of the air craft carrier he took off from as being the "Natoma" before he plummeted to his death in the battle of Iwo Jima. He even described how his plane was hit in the engine causing it to catch on fire and go down quickly in the water below. He also told them that he had a friend on the same boat named Jack Larsen. It turned out, that there was a ship called the USS Natoma Bay, which did take part in World War II at Iwo Jima, and a pilot named Jack Larsen witnessed how the plane he was flying next to was hit, describing it exactly how this little boy in Louisiana told his parents it happened.

Understand, most of this knowledge was information that could only be confirmed by military records. You should also keep in mind, the internet has not been around for 40 or 50 years like this study has. This isn't a story of a parent compiling information to make their child seem special. Nor is it a child or parent who could have had any way of learning these facts at all, much less before the age of 6, as is apparently the oldest age of recall, when these children begin to let go of their past life and embrace their present one.

After 50 years of studying these kinds of cases, following the children through their lives as they divulged more and more factual information, most of which could only be confirmed through government records, there came a surprising conclusion. The research team at the University of Virginia has concluded that the concept of reincarnation is a TRUE human condition! Reincarnation is the only explanation that fits all the criteria discovered and researched. To me, at least, this proves reincarnation is real through a study covering 5 decades and 3000 cases, and from what I would consider to be well educated men supported by a very credible institution.

This is no joke; reincarnation is the reality of mankind's existence, whether you can believe it or not. We aren't just given one chance to get it right or suffer the consequences for the rest of eternity. We work at it UNTIL we get it right, even if that takes an eternity. The thing is, however, reincarnation is also not as it seems, or as many assume.

To illustrate this, let me just give you some food for thought. Ask yourself this. How can reincarnation be a condition of living past lives if there is no past in the spiritual realm? When we die from one life, our consciousness would be living in the spiritual realm only, which means we would be living in eternal time, where everything is in the present. What if it would suit the purpose for our next life better to live 500 years before we died in our last life? Wouldn't it be as possible for our soul to choose any period in our frame of time, since it is coming from a place where all time is in the present? I'm telling you, nothing is as it seems, least of all those things we assume fit in the boxes of our own design.

Spiritual Curiosity

I continued to try to pursue a successful computer software business for maybe 6 months or so after my "wake up call", but I was forcing it, going against my destiny from that point forward, which can only be seen clearly in hindsight. Even though I did everything I could to maintain my computer business, the Australian theft mentality made that impossible for me.

After discovering a major Australian Government owned company stole my report generating software and a company I contracted for tried to steal my library of intricate routines right off my own home computer, a combined total of more than 17 years of work, I'd had enough of the theft mentality in Australia. But, when they stole every copy of a customizable accounting software I'd written thinking it was theft proof due to the service required to customize it, I was devastated. I'd put all my hopes and my last dollar into this trade show, bringing all my inventory including detailed instruction manuals, and they stole it all out of our vehicle as we were packing up to go.

Out of money, out of inventory, and out of tolerance for people who had no respect for the hard work that goes into developing computer software, I was done. Three strikes and you're out, sort of speak. It was just not worth the stress of it in a country that thrives on theft. I was so overwhelmed by it all, that I didn't even want to come near a computer for quite a while. It was time for me to find something else to do with my life.

Finding My Path

Not sure what to do with myself, having given up on my computer profession forever, I decided to dust off my favorite craft supplies and do some Indian beadwork just to fill my time while I figured out my next move. As I was working away stringing beads, contemplating what career I should pursue next, my thoughts went to how wonderful it would be to make a living doing Indian beadwork.

The problem is; beadwork is way too time consuming to make any money at it, so this wasn't the first time I'd realized, that selling finished beadwork was never an option worth pursuing. Revisiting this dream, however, allowed a brilliant brainstorm to come to mind. What if I were to create beadwork kits and let other people spend the time required to finish the project? Hence, my Native American craft supply business was born, and ironically, in a country on the other side of the world from Native Americans.

Australians barely knew what Indian beadwork even was, much less how to do it. To overcome this obvious obstacle, my kits had to be designed in a way that would teach them the craft, while also illustrating the symbolism that goes into developing a beadwork pattern. What really surprised me was how receptive the Australian crafters were to this new craft. It was becoming a resounding success!! I wasn't making tons of money, of course, but I was making a small contribution to the household and was able to slowly grow my business at the same time. Most importantly, I was finally doing something I truly enjoyed doing, which nobody could pilfer or even wanted to steal.

As I told you, it was exactly 20 years from my Angel message to that spiritual "wake up call". Since I now understand how spirit works, I can see clearly in hindsight that the plan for my "predestiny" was falling into place from the moment I dusted off my old beading supplies. There was a surprise waiting for me surrounding this new venture I set out on. It turns out; the Australians looked to Native Americans as spiritual leaders, and to Native American beliefs as profound spiritual wisdom.

The full realization of this didn't hit me until I decided to open a shop in a small strip mall close to our house, and was finally able to meet my customers. Before that, I'd mainly sold my kits wholesale to other shops, or directly through mail order. Again, at this point in my story, the internet was barely born and definitely not something anyone used for shopping. I had to promote my kits the old school way, by advertising in magazines or knocking on doors myself. That's why I wanted to open a store, because it seemed easier. It was in my small strip mall store where my spiritual education really began.

Finding Your Purpose
There is a lesson in this I'd like to mention quickly. Most people think they are on the path they should be on when they are doing something that excites them or makes their heart sing. Even though this is often the case, I think it's important to realize, that it's not always your favorite thing to do or where your talents lie that coincides with the plan your soul had in mind for you. If I were only pursuing what makes my heart sing, I would still be a computer programmer.

I've been known to work 36 hours straight without so much as a dinner break programming computer software, and I couldn't have done that if it weren't something I was passionate about. I loved it so much I would lose myself in it, time would disappear as I relished at the challenges of writing the intricate software routines. But, the only thing that work I loved was bringing me was heartache, as people took advantage of me and stole from me. It was when I was taking a break from what made my heart sing, that the spiritual influences began to show me a new path, one I could not even imagine for myself. Of course, I also enjoy all Indian crafts, but not to the degree and with the same passion I felt for computer programming.

What you should really look for, to know whether you are on the best path for your life journey or not, is how life is treating you overall. Are you being appreciated for your long hours doing what you love to do, or are people becoming jealous over the extra income or angry over your absence from their lives? Are good things happening in your life, or are there distractions trying to throw you off your game? If something or someone is making your life miserable, while you are only trying to do what you love so much, then perhaps your passion is not your calling.

It's not just about following your heart strings, because you may not be able to learn what you need to learn from that career or life choice. It may just be what you did in your last life, which is what makes it feel so comfortable and why you are so good at it. But, if you already lived it, then you already learned from it, so it may not be where your best growth for this life will come from.

As it turned out, my computer skills have come in very handy in all my future endeavors, even in writing this book, so understand, everything does happen for a reason. It's just that we shouldn't allow our own selfish cravings cloud us from the whispers directing us to our true calling.

Seeking Spiritual Insight

Ever since my "wake up call", I had a general yearning for some spiritual insight. I was really wondering how these things were happening to me, what force was causing them to happen. What is it, that is out there where our eyes can't see, and what does it want from me? Since reading books never was my thing, that avenue for learning didn't even occur to me.

Once I settled into my Indian crafts shop, I began looking for a psychic. After all, it was the psychic readers at that small "psychic fair" who started me down this curious voyage, so I wanted to learn more about what they could tell me. I was really wondering what that last "wake up call" was trying to wake me up to. What was it that I'd been trying to achieve in all those lives he'd said I've lived before? What am I supposed to achieve in this life? Where do I start?

The White Witch

I was finally introduced to a lady who had been doing psychic and other spiritual work most of her life. As a result of her highly esteemed reputation and decades of experience, her price was extremely high. I was willing to pay the price for someone genuine, so I went to her for a reading ready to pay for her expertise.

But then, to my surprise, the tables turned. She saw something in me, and offered to give me a free reading if I would read her in return. What? I'd never even looked at a set of Tarot cards before this. In fact, I didn't even know what they were, since the only other readers in my life, at that small "psychic fair", weren't using Tarot cards. I told her I had no idea how to do it, but she assured me I had "the gift".

Entering this mysterious realm of the unseen already had me very nervous, which increased substantially when she referred to herself as a "white witch". I've always had a fear of witches resulting from a series of dreams I had as a young child. This lady, along with the title of "witch" she was obviously proud of, gave me the creeps, the way she seemed to know more about me than I knew about myself. Still, I wanted to learn about spiritual matters bad enough to follow her lead with caution.

She proceeded to give me a reading, which was full of information I wasn't sure about. For one thing, she told me I had an admirer. In fact, I found out later I did, but I just told him I was happily married, and that was the end of that. The point is; her information was accurate, but mostly unknown to me at the time of the reading.

Just so you know, another thing she told me, which has not yet become a reality, was that she saw me standing on several stages talking about my "work". She said, on that first meeting, that she saw me going to several different cities across Australia, but on another day and another reading, she saw me traveling all over the world sharing my "work" on a stage in front of 100's of people. This made no sense to me at the time, since the only work I knew anything about was computers and how to make a dreamcatcher. Obviously, that has changed, since of course, my work is spiritual now, so only time will tell if this prediction comes true.

After she finished my reading, she still wanted me to read her, so I used her cards to give her my first reading ever. For those who don't realize this, psychic readers are

Spiritual Curiosity

usually unable to read themselves with any accuracy. They simply have too much invested in the reading to put their own preferences and fears aside and allow their instincts to do the work without their assumptions clouding the true message. Everyone thinks a psychic should know everything, but those kinds of comments only insult their integrity, because the reality is so very far removed from that "joke".

Since I had no idea how to even begin a reading, I simply followed the same method of laying out the cards she had used, clueless of each individual card's meaning. She told me to just feel what they were trying to tell me. So, I looked closely at the pictures on the cards and allowed my instincts to form a story in my mind. Low and behold, to my surprise, she told me I was completely accurate in everything I said. I was even able to give her information she had been wondering about. Who knew? I'm a psychic?

My Psychic Gift

It turns out, I am pretty psychically gifted, which leads me to another story I'd have to call a spiritual experience only because of how amazingly accurate I can be with this gift. I purchased some Tarot cards for myself to hone my newly found skills. For your information, however, I found out later that these cards work best for you if you receive them as gift, so I had to sleep with them under my pillow to help them tune into my energy.

There's actually a lot of work involved in memorizing the meanings of all those cards, especially since you have to learn their meaning whether they land right side up or reversed, since each carries a very different meaning. Then, to make the task even harder, the cards can have an altered meaning according to the surrounding cards, so it can get very complicated. Once you know their meaning, you then have to let that schooling go and learn how to allow your instincts to lead you.

One day, when I was getting the meanings of the cards down pretty good, and figuring out how to use my instincts in the process, we had our best friends over for dinner. Just for the heck of it, for the "fun" of it all, my friend asked me to do some readings for them. The wife wanted me to read her husband right there at the dining table with the four of us watching the outcome together. Well, her husband wanted no part of it and tried every way out of this idea he could think of. But, we convinced him it was just for fun, that it was nothing anyone was taking seriously.

I'll never forget that reading. Right away, I started to see some serious fortunes falling in place before my eyes, but nothing I dared say out loud in front of everyone. At first, I thought maybe I was imagining things, but as the cards continued to lay down adding perfectly to the picture that was forming, I realized there was something to this. I even started to wonder if maybe this was why he didn't want to be read, because what I was seeing was not something he would have wanted disclosed.

Since this was supposed to be all in "fun", I did not state one word out loud of what I was seeing. None of this information would have been any fun for anybody, so I just sat there and told him a pack of lies. Cool, that was fun, at least for them, but the vision I'd gotten was haunting me.

This lady was my very best friend in the world, people we'd lived with for months while we got ourselves established in this new country. But, what I was seeing was literally the demise of their 20 year marriage. I pictured a dark haired woman in my mind, whom he was currently having an affair with. I saw him leaving his wife and moving to America, with the hope that this dark haired woman would come with him.

Even though he was Australian born, he would be able to move to America with ease, since he'd fought as an American in the Vietnam War. In fact, he'd fought in the same outfit as my husband, the "Herd", or to us laymen, the 173rd Airborne Division. It was a choice they'd given him when he was busted with an expired visa, to either be deported permanently, or fight in our Army. The bonus of that latter choice was that he would be rewarded with the same veteran benefits our soldiers receive if he were to ever move here permanently.

He loved America, and had been wanting to move here for a very long time. His American wife, however, did not want to move back, which had always been a sore spot between them. She talked him into raising their kids in the country they were born in, especially since Australia is a much safer environment for kids than America ever was. Problem is, those kids were grown now, so his obligation to his children was fulfilled.

This vision of their future was too strong in me to keep it to myself. I knew in my heart, that her husband was having an affair. Now what do I do? I decided it would be wrong of me to keep this to myself, as her best friend, and as the spiritual person I was becoming. There had to be a reason the clearest reading I've ever experienced happened that night, so to keep it to myself, I felt, was the wrong thing to do.

The next time I saw her, I sat her down and told her every detail I saw, which was quite extensive, but of course, with the clarification that this was only a reading from an inexperienced reader. I just had to tell her, but couldn't guarantee its accuracy, even though in my heart I felt it probably was true. She was shocked by the thought of it, and swore I had to be wrong. Her husband would never do that to her. They'd been through too much together for him to do that. I was completely fine with her assessment, so we just left it at that.

It wasn't long, however, before his affair was exposed. It was a dark haired woman he'd met down at the local bar, which I also saw. He finally owned up to the truth with his wife, because he wanted to move to America and take this woman with him, just as I'd seen. I'd told her the woman wouldn't go in the end, and within a couple more months, that is exactly what ended up happening.

With it all said and done, it was truly astounding how accurate I was. I hadn't missed a single point, so my friend came to me for more readings. I felt obligated to help her through this in any way I could, but again, she didn't like what the cards were telling me. So, she would repeatedly ask me over and over again for another reading, in hopes they would change, but they never did. The sad news was; the couple would never get back together, that he would never move back to Australia, and she would only see him one more time, when he wanted money from her.

It was about a year later when he came to Australia for a "visit". She was so excited to see him again, hoping he would come back to her. But again, my readings were spot on, because he only came to ask her to put a 2nd mortgage on the house so he could have the money from it. She loved him so much she accommodated him, and gave him virtually all 20 years of equity from their house, landing her with a new mortgage to pay when it had almost been paid off.

As sad as that experience was in my psychic career, it was obvious I had psychic abilities, but it wasn't a gift I was too excited about. A gift is a gift, however, and I felt ignoring that gift would have been wrong somehow. I've since learned that one gift may only be one aspect of your greater gift.

As I was practicing reading myself to learn the cards and their meanings, I received three messages from the cards, on three very separate occasions, designed to teach me this lesson. They were telling me, that being a card reader was not my calling. Notice, as usual, it took me three times to finally hear the message, but once I did, I avoided ever reading cards again. To this day, I won't do it for money or for friends, and especially not for "fun".

Spiritual Visitors

My small shop, where I sold my Indian craft kits and supplies along with some finished Indian arts, seemed to attract spiritual people to me like a magnet. Seeking out the white witch never gave me any real answers and it only started me down the wrong path as a psychic reader. So, I decided it wasn't helpful to have others tell you what they perceived of your life. Like I said in the introduction of this book, I was not the one who pursued a spiritual life, it pursued me. I learned early on, I have to wait for Spirit to call on me, not the other way around.

The Psychic Lady

One example of the attraction my shop had to spiritual people was a very old and very spiritually gifted lady who became a regular visitor to my shop. One of my employees encouraged her, but my initial sentiment was not so welcoming, since she never spent any money and only seemed to waste our time as we kindly tolerated her. The more time went on, however, I began to discover the overwhelming spiritual gifts this lady had, so much so, that most people of the neighborhood avoided her due to her "strange visions" and the like.

Before long, I grew to love that lady very much, as we spent hours together almost every day just chatting about Spirit. I believe I was one of the few people on the planet she shared her story of spousal abuse with, which reached far beyond the imagination, horrible mistreatment I respect her too much to repeat. She suffered such horrendous abuse, that I believe her spiritual gifts were brought to the surface as a result. She would have had to go elsewhere in her mind just to maintain some sort of sanity. Regardless of what tuned her in, her gifts were truly profound, and she never asked for money for her insights from anybody.

One of my favorite stories she told me was of a time when she was just walking down the sidewalk and passed a young man from the neighborhood. As she passed by him, she got a very strong message from Spirit about him, so she went back to him to give him the message. She told him it was very important that he does NOT take the bridge to work that coming Friday, that his life would be in danger if he did. Of course, the neighbors told him to ignore her, but he decided to give her the benefit of the doubt, and simply stayed home from work that day.

Sure enough, that morning, right at the time of day when he would have been driving over the bridge to go to work, the bridge collapsed killing several people. She saved that young man's life that day, but the neighbors and even her own children still shunned her, fearful, I believe, of her spiritual connection. I, on the other hand, was proud to have her as a friend.

One day, early on in our relationship, she offered to give me a free reading, just for fun. It was during that sit down reading that I got a firsthand glimpse at how spiritually gifted this lady truly was. She told me a lot about myself that nobody else could have known, including some things I'd even forgotten about. She reminded me of a time in my youth I'd spent singing with the "Up With People" organization, which was when I was 15-16 years old.

She didn't know the name of the group, but described it as a "singing and dancing group". That description didn't help me recall it right away, but then she said, "Not really dancing, but making moves in unison", as she began mimicking the moves we would make. That's when I remembered that experience, because she had the moves down exactly. Impressive, but she was far from done impressing me with her gifts that day.

Not only did she know I was in the singing group I'd long forgotten about, but she even knew where I stood in the lineup and also where my best friend stood. We were all positioned according to our height, and wore different colored dresses that made sense in that lineup, so we always had to maintain the same position on stage. I'm fairly tall, so I stood in the 2nd row near the center, while my best friend was very short prompting her position as dead center of the first row.

What really astounded me is when she described my long lost best friend in great detail, from her short height and dark hair to the scar on the tip of her nose. She explained that it was my friend telling her these things, and that she was with me often. This astounded me, because, you see, my friend had died when she was only 16 years old. This lady had no way of knowing any of that. Those are the kinds of things that convinced me of how accurate she was with spiritual messages. There is still much more I learned from this lady, which I will tell you about when the time is right to do so.

My India Guru

Another example of Spirit coming to me in the same shop was a man I can only describe as an India Guru, evidenced by the turban he wore on his head and his obvious India accent. Without saying a word, he handed me a small card, and on it, he was asking me if I would like to have a palm reading done. I asked him how much, and he shook his head to indicate he didn't want any money. I insisted on paying him $10, and would have paid him more if I could have afforded it, because $10 was extremely cheap for any sort of reading in Australia or anywhere.

The thing I found interesting right away, is my employee desperately wanted a reading too. But even as she was begging for his attention, he never even gave her a 2nd glance throughout his visit. It was as if Spirit had sent him specifically for my sake to come help me get some answers. He was focused entirely and only on me.

A lot of information was discussed in the reading that day, so much that I worried I would forget what he told me. When I expressed my concerns, he said I would recall everything he'd said when the need to remember presented itself. There was actually too much discussed to include it all here. Since a lot of what he had to say is related to different topics I want to talk about in this book, I will refer back to him whenever his information becomes relevant in chapters to come. Still, there are some things worth mentioning now.

One thing you should understand is where I was coming from at this point in my life. I actually did NOT consider myself spiritual at all when I opened this small shop, one Aussies assumed was a very spiritual shop. Since

I was still not yet tuned in enough to understand the difference between being spiritual and being religious and had long ago put religion behind me forever, I considered myself very non-spiritual.

The first thing my Guru told me, even before we sat down to do the reading, is that "spiritual success" was the most important thing to me. He was giving me the three things that I considered as most important in my life, counting spiritual success as number 1, relationships as number 2, and good health as number 3. Right away, before he could even tell me my numbers 2 or 3, I started arguing with him. I swore to him he was very wrong about that first one, that the last thing I cared about was anything spiritual (meaning anything religious in my mind).

Usually, when you adamantly argue with any psychic, telling them they definitely have it wrong, they will reconsider their interpretation of the message and change the way they are presenting it to you. Not my Guru. He insisted without the slightest hesitation that my number 1 priority in life was spiritual success.

That's the way he worded it, spiritual success, and he told me I'd achieve it too, without ever defining it. Obviously, he knew me better than I knew myself. All these years later, I couldn't agree with him more. Spiritual success is by far the most important thing in the world to me, but I'm still waiting and hoping to achieve the success he promised.

The next thing he did is show me my first miracle. When we first sat down to do the palm reading, he handed me a piece of paper folded so many times it was only 1/2 inch square or smaller. He told me to hold it firmly in my left hand throughout the reading, stressing how important it was to not let it go until the reading was completely done.

Then he pulled out another small piece of paper and pen, and wrote down my answers to 3 simple questions, my current age, favorite flower, and I think the last question was my mother's name.

Leaving that paper unfolded, he put it in the little Hindu book he was carrying and proceeded with the palm reading, using only my right hand. When the reading was done, he told me to open the folded paper I still held in my left hand. Low and behold, it was the same paper he had put in the back of his book, which was now blank. It had all the answers to my questions on it, which he had asked me AFTER I placed that paper in my left hand!! I believe he performed this little miracle to prove to me the importance of his visit and accuracy of his words, which by the way, to this date have been 100% correct. But again, much of what he said is still unfolding.

Red Feather
Another regular customer, who turned out to be very spiritual, gravitated to my shop like a bee to honey. It was all the Native American arts and crafts that called to the heart strings of this young man, who liked to call himself Red Feather. He would, at least, buy something once in a while, but he didn't have a lot of money, and mostly, he just wanted to be in the environment of my shop. He said it felt like home to him, and over time he slowly opened up to me and told me his story.

He started out telling me that most people think he's crazy, but he knows he's not crazy. He'd told his parents all about this stuff, and their reaction was to worry about his sanity, but this young man seemed entirely sane to me. It's just that his story is a bit out there, but as I've grown over the years, I realize now, his story is not even all that unusual. In fact, it's very much like those children who were scrutinized by the University of Virginia for their 50 year study on reincarnation. He knew he was a reincarnated American Indian, but in all his life nobody would believe him.

His story starts out with a memory most of us don't have, being able to recall his infant years and with some recollection of even being in his mother's womb. There are people who do have a memory of such things, even though it is rare, but Red Feather's memory goes even further back, to a memory of his prior life.

The sad thing is, if someone would have believed him early on he would have probably been able to release his prior life and embrace this new one. Just like those young children in the 50 year study, he needed some validation so he could move on. Instead, he was stuck in the past trying to resolve what he knew as a memory, while others who loved him were telling him there was something mentally wrong with him.

He would always try to come when I was alone in the shop, because he was very shy about his story. He would test me with little tidbits here and there until he could trust that I had an open mind on spiritual matters and my heart was compassionate enough to hear him out. I am naturally always first inclined to be a skeptic, but with an open mind to some proof. Besides, he so desperately needed to share his story with someone who wouldn't belittle him over it. I've been through enough judgment in my life to hear him out with some empathy in my heart, even if his story was a bit strange.

With my acceptance of him, I watched a change slowly come over him. Finally, for the first time in his life, someone was willing to hear him out and even believe his story. Everybody needs somebody to accept them for

Vision Of Truth

exactly who they are. Already, my new path was helping someone, and without any effort on my part. It was the most natural thing in the world for me, to have compassion for someone standing alone in the world. At the same time I was helping him, he was helping me without either of us realizing it. He was introducing me to some spiritual truths I eventually grew to understand truly are our reality.

One of the spiritual truths he taught me is that we all have Spirit Guides helping us find our way throughout our lives. Most people have heard of this term, "Spirit Guide", but some prefer to consider them Angels guiding us rather than Spirit Guides. It doesn't matter what you want to call them, as long as you realize that we do all have spiritual guidance helping us at all times, and we can call on them for that help at any and every moment in our lives.

What we need to realize is they need our request for help, since our free will is always the top priority to Spirit. We are always the one in charge. Therefore, with complete respect for our choices, they guide us quietly. They might place subtle thoughts in our mind or stir up our gut feelings, what we call our intuition, to keep us heading in the right direction. Of course, we always have the choice of ignoring those subtle suggestions, as too many of us most often do.

Red Feather was the first to explain this concept of Spirit Guides to me, informing me that we all have at least one Spirit Guide, and sometimes many, who guide and protect us throughout our lives. In addition to that, other guides will come to our aid who are better equipped to help in a particular situation in our life, like calling in the plumber when you have a leak. I've also learned since, that sometimes we may be getting ready to make a major shift in our lives, which requires a whole new team of guides to come help us. During that transition of losing our old guides and getting accustomed to the new, we may have the feeling of being very alone and may even get depressed over the loss without understanding why we are feeling so down.

Red Feather told me his guide's name was Kicking Bird, of course, an American Indian name. It is very often that our guides are our relatives from long ago, so this is not as strange as it may seem. What hit me, in this part of his story, is that a crazy person would have picked a well-known Indian as their Spirit Guide name, like Crazy Horse, or Geronimo. Nobody has ever heard of an Indian named Kicking Bird, or at least I hadn't. It added credibility to his story in my mind, which helped me keep my mind open. Still, I remained on guard as the skeptic I naturally am, yet without letting him know that to protect his feelings.

Every time he would come into my shop he would tell me some kind of news his guide, Kicking Bird, had told him. It was becoming more and more believable with time and with the news from his guide making sense. Then, one day, still not sure how much of this I believed, I told him how lucky he was to have that connection with his guide. My intentions were mainly to give him a boost of confidence, but then he surprised me by offering a proof I could not deny.

He said anyone could do it, if they wanted to, and asked me if I wanted him to see if he could connect with my Spirit Guide. I was surprised at the offer, and asked him if he could do that. He said he wasn't sure, but he could ask Kicking Bird if he could achieve this with his help. I was open to the idea, since there weren't many customers that day, so he went to the back of my shop to connect with Kicking Bird and make the request. When he came out, he seemed to be in a partial trance like state, as he announced that

Kicking Bird was going to help him connect with my Spirit Guide.

He sat down next to me, was quiet for a moment, and then his demeanor changed and his voice was a bit deeper. He was now speaking for my guide, as if my guide had taken over his voice. In fact, what he was doing is channeling, which I was completely unfamiliar with at the time, but more on that topic later. I was still very skeptical about all this, so I was going to test this scenario to the max.

I no longer remember all the details of a dream I'd had just prior to this day, but I did at the time and figured that would be a good test. So, I asked him what my dream was trying to tell me without describing the dream to him in anyway. To my surprise, he described my dream to me and explained its meaning, and even pointed out that he knew I was testing him. He said I could find the proof I was seeking in his story, which I didn't understand at the time.

Then, he started to tell me his story. My guide's name is Two Dogs, again an Indian name I've never heard of, but definitely an American Indian who lived as a warrior. As another test, I asked him what he wore, since I figured I knew more accurately what an Indian warrior would wear than an Australian who called himself Red Feather. He referred to his clothing as normal attire of an Indian warrior, which were buckskin pants and shirts most of the time, since he lived in the north. He also said he wore a headband with two feathers hanging down.

Then he said something that really surprised me. He said he wanted to thank me for the honor of asking him to be my Spirit Guide. He said he was amazed, that someone like me would ask someone like him to carry out such an important job. I asked what he meant, what makes me so important or him so unimportant for him to say that? He said he'd lived a shameful life, and he went on to explain what the two feathers hanging down represented. He said he'd copped coup on two separate occasions, where he had mortally wounded the Indian he'd been in conflict with both times. That was why the feathers hung down, because they were worn as a badge of shame.

I understood what he was referring to, even though Red Feather didn't, from an interest in my own Indian heritage. To cop coup is to touch an enemy warrior, usually with a coup stick, but without harming them or getting hurt yourself. The bravery was in having the guts to get that close to an enemy with respect and without fear. Each coup (pronounced koo) earned an Indian warrior a feather, which is how headdresses came to be. Regardless of whether the coup was successful in leaving both parties unharmed or not, the warrior always earned a feather. The shame or honor in the deed was in how the feather was to be worn from that day forward.

He went on to say he was banished from his tribe for it on the 2nd time, because his actions were a cowardly act, not worthy of a warrior in his tribe. He told us the name of the Indian he actually killed on the 2nd coup was "Spotted Bear" or something like that. He said he was a brother of someone in his tribe, and that it was an accident or he was misidentified. I can't remember it all now, but this is where it gets freaky. I could find out those details for you if I could get to the library, because this story is documented in history.

It was a few days later, when Red Feather came into my shop with a book in his hand. He said he felt driven to go the library and research this. Sure enough, there it was, exactly as my guide had described. The Indian he had killed was somewhat famous, it appears, which is why it was documented, even though not so famous that I'd ever heard of him. There it was, undeniable proof written boldly in black and white to help me get beyond my skepticism. My guide had told me, remember, that I would find the proof I needed in his story. That is exactly what we did find, even documented proof.

Spirit providing me with proof was a common thread throughout many of my experiences, as if Spirit was trying to help me get past my skepticism. I was given proof every time I needed it, until finally I did accept Spirit fully. Even though I still approach most things with a skeptical attitude, I do know now, that anything is possible, which allows me to hear it out always with an open mind waiting for the proof. That is also all I can ask of you readers. The proof will come if we are paying attention and remain open enough to see it.

Finding Purpose

With everything that had happened to me, a white man transforming into an Indian, having a conversation with an angel, and the like, you'd think I would start to realize Spirit had something planned for me, that I had a specific purpose in this life. Nope, not me, since I hadn't yet even grasped the concept of anyone having a reason for living beyond what they planned for themselves. I'd been shown I had a predestiny as a child, but that idea didn't yet sit right with me, and it surely wasn't a commitment I was supposed to do something about. It never dawned on me that there could be a purpose I wasn't aware of.

Even though I'd experienced the all-knowingness in the highest spiritual realm where I'd taken on a responsibility I still had to fulfill, I just muddled through life as if all that was a forgotten mystery. It took someone specifically telling me what my purpose was before I even began to grasp there was such a thing as a preplanned function I was supposed to engage in. Like I said, Spirit pursued me while I was just fumbling along like a lost lamb.

My Divine Purpose

It was the psychic lady who woke me up a little to this possibility of a divine purpose. She was visiting me at my house one day, helping me pack for the move we were about to make to another part of Australia. She suddenly stopped cold in her tracks in a stare, as she began describing what she was seeing in her vision. She said there was an Indian relative of mine who was dancing in front of her giving her a message for me.

I asked what he was wearing, since my first inclination is always to test. She said he was in normal buckskin attire, nothing fancy, and a small headdress with 2 feathers hanging down at the temple. Immediately, my little test was passed with flying colors, since this is the exact same attire my guide had described himself as wearing, which this lady had no knowledge of. She was telling me he is a relative, rather than my guide, but I think he may have been both.

Anyway, she began to describe a ceremony she was witnessing when the stupid phone rang. I wanted to just let it ring, but then the loud ringing was just as much of a distraction. I answered it and got rid of them as soon as I could. Through it all, she continued to voice what she was seeing, but I couldn't listen to both her and the caller, which was really frustrating. I was very relieved that after the phone call she was still having the vision, and acted as if she never even heard the phone at all.

She was still describing the ceremony she said several people were having with me, saying that I was leading them through it. I'm sorry to say, I missed most of the details of that ceremony, but everything happens for a reason, including that phone call. All I know is there were a bunch of tents and teepees with campfires in front of them

Finding Purpose

and people standing around their own fires. She said everyone was raising their hands into the air.

Then suddenly she realized what the purpose of this ceremony was, saying it was meant to help save lost souls. She was very delighted when she announced, "its working!!" I was glad to hear the ceremony was working, which meant some lost souls were going to be saved. But, I didn't know what to think about me leading the ceremony, or how it would work, or even how a soul gets lost in the first place.

Then suddenly she gasped in surprise, and she said, "Oh my God, Kathy, this is your purpose in life, YOU ARE HERE TO SAVE LOST SOULS!!!" Wow!! Really? What does that even mean? At the time, I was imagining the ceremony as being a means of saving the souls of people who had died, our hands being up in the air and all, where we imagine dead people to be. What can I say; I was still an infant in my spiritual awakening at the time. What I can tell you now, is our loved ones are right there with us, just in a different dimension, but not up in the clouds somewhere.

It was some years later, long after we had returned to America, that a revelation came to me. All I remember is immediately sharing the news with my husband who was with me on a road trip at the time it happened. The revelation was informing me, that I am here to save the souls of the LIVING. Her message was not about saving dead souls, but about saving lost souls while they are still ALIVE. I do understand now, she was right, that is what I am here to do. At least, that is what I hope to achieve with my spiritual work.

Her message was spot on, and that work only begins with this book, and will continue as my primary purpose throughout this series of books, starting with my next book,

<u>Echoes From Spirit</u>. Even though it took me many years to understand her message, the fact that I had a purpose at all was very important to me at the time. It gave me a reason to continue my spiritual quest. Heck, it gave me a reason for living at all. That little old lady saved my soul, or at least had a part in what started me down my spiritual path towards my true purpose.

Three Messages

The next story I am about to tell you illustrates, that indeed, Spirit did choose me for a specific purpose. Be very clear on one thing before I tell you this story. These three messages not only were not solicited by me, but were not even believed by me until finally the third message convinced me it must be real. I simply cannot ignore this depth of proof, that indeed, I have some work to do for humanity, even as I still wait for that work to begin so many years later.

The Psychic Lady

The first of these three messages from Spirit came through my psychic lady friend again. It was during another sit down reading we did, long after I knew how in touch she clearly was with Spirit. This reading was different though, since I had no idea what to do with this bizarre news. I had to believe she was receiving this message from Spirit, but none of it made any sense to me at the time.

The first thing she did is ask me if I knew anybody who was pregnant. I didn't, and told her so, but she insisted I did know this lady, or at least I would know her soon. She said it's also possible that the lady doesn't know she's pregnant yet, since this is a very young fetus she has to tell me about.

Then it got serious, when she informed me that the fetus is a girl who will come to me when she is older. She said it's very important that I open my heart to this girl when she comes. To stress the importance, she repeated, that I need to be sure to open my heart completely to this girl and teach her everything I know. She said this little girl has a very important job to do in this world and I need to teach her everything I know to help her achieve it. She hesitated... then she said, "Oh my God, Kathy, this girl is the next messiah!"

Oh brother, that seems a bit much. What am I supposed to do with that? All I could think of at the time was that I didn't have anything to teach anybody, much less a messiah! I didn't know what to think. I had to just blow it off, and told her I didn't know anyone who was pregnant, so none of it was making any sense. She said it should make sense later, and moved on in her reading.

My Competitor

There's more to this messiah story, but it didn't come until after we made that first move to a more touristy part of Australia, the Sunshine Coast, where I thought my products would sell better. As before, unsolicited spiritual experiences and messages continued to come my way in this new part of the country. There were even more spiritually attuned people in this touristy area than in the big city of Melbourne we had come from. This is when I really began to open my mind to all this spiritual stuff. After all, I was in the spiritual business, since that's how Australians perceived a Native American store.

I had some competition in this part of the world, however, as surprising as that may seem. Dream catchers were a big thing, for example, and available at several stores in the area, but I was the only full blown Native

American store on the beach walk. I'd heard of a competitor somewhere in a mall several miles away, and everyone kept telling me I should go check out her store. One day I was able to get away from my store long enough to do just that.

I was checking out the Native American corner in her generally spiritual shop, when a lady came up and tapped me on the shoulder. She said there was an Indian chief standing behind me with an important message he wanted her to tell me. Assuming she was the owner, my competitor, I felt an immediate animosity towards her. My opinion of who this lady may have been was actually clouding my ability to accept her message. So at the time, I was very skeptical, even cynical towards this lady and whatever she had to tell me.

She proceeded to state her message anyway to my closed mind, trying her best to make it very clear how important the message was. The first thing she did in response to my initial test, was describe what the Indian chief was wearing. She said he wore a full headdress with 2 rows of feathers reaching all the way to the ground. That description of any Indian's attire hit me as the typical way an Australian would picture an American Indian. I figured if any Indian had a message for me, it would be my guide who only wore 2 feathers in his headdress. Right away, I felt vindicated in discrediting her information in my mind. She had failed my test miserably.

But, then it got spooky. She stated word for word EXACTLY what the psychic lady had told me some 4 or 5 months prior in another town over 1000 miles away. She told me that a little girl, still in the womb, was going to come to me when she was old enough, and that I needed to open my heart to her completely. She also repeated it, just as the psychic lady had done, telling me I needed be sure I opened my heart completely and teach her everything I knew. She continued by telling me this little girl has a very important job to do in this world, and I have to help her learn what she needs to know for her journey. Okay, now this is getting weird, I thought.

Being the skeptic I am, I set out to test her with some more questions, starting with whether I knew the mother or not. She thought for a second, and then said, "Yes, you do, or at least you will know her soon". Then I asked how important this job was, that this little girl was supposed to do. She said it was VERY VERY important. I asked, "As important as maybe being a messiah might be?" I figured she would pooh pooh that huge exaggeration of the importance of a job anyone would have to do, and she would sink herself under the pressure of that question. She paused for a second as she checked her sources. Then, with a surprised look on her face, she said, "wow, yes, that is her purpose, or at least her job is that important".

All the way back to my store, I was torn over this message. The Indian was dressed wrong, but the message was exactly the same. Still, I knew nobody who was pregnant, and I didn't trust the lady in that store. I didn't know why she would do that, or how, but I just couldn't accept it. It was just all too bizarre, and so, I threw it away like yesterday's garbage.

I told my husband about it, and the girl running my store while I was gone, and they both thought it sounded pretty credible, but I refused to let it in. They both seemed disappointed in my choice to ignore the message, but just because I ignored it didn't mean I forgot it. I actually have a very good memory, which has served me well, and this was way too bizarre to leave my memory any time soon.

My Customer

That wasn't good enough for Spirit, however. I was meant to hear this message loud and clear, and believe it, come hell or high water. The third time it came from a completely different person who knew nothing of the other two people or of the messages I'd already received. And again, it was completely unsolicited by me and from a person I didn't even know was a psychic. She was a customer in my store. She said she'd been there a couple times before, but I didn't recognize her, so perhaps one of my employees had waited on her.

I was measuring out some lengths of leather lacing she wanted when she became startled by something she was seeing. She said there was an Indian with a full headdress standing behind me. Remembering the competitor lady's message, I asked her to describe the headdress. She defined it as having two rows of feathers reaching all the way to the ground, exactly as the last lady had portrayed. She continued, "He wants you to know that he is your relative, and that you should know that you are Cherokee". With this statement, I had to open my mind a bit, since it gave some credibility to why a different Indian would be bringing me a message.

You see, I had been wondering about my heritage, since everyone in America seems to claim they have Cherokee blood in their family history. Our family also believes we are Cherokee, but I'd always had my doubts. My Great Great Grandmother, on her death bed, when she finally admitted for the first time that she was a full blooded Indian, had told my uncle something confusing this issue. When she made this grand announcement, he asked her what tribe she was from. He told me her response sounded like gibberish to him, but it started with the letter "O" and had a "J" in it somewhere.

The "Ojibwa" Indian nation fits the bill perfectly, in my mind, so I always wondered if we were Ojibwa rather than Cherokee, especially since we were all from Ohio, where the Ojibwa were strong. Once we'd returned to America armed with this message from my relative, that I am Cherokee, I did a search in the Cherokee rolls for my Great Great Grandmother's name and I did find it, so it appears that part of this customer's message was correct. I am part Cherokee.

I continued measuring her leather lacing, as I responded to her message, letting her know it was interesting, because I'd been wondering about my heritage. I thought that was the end of it, but then she started again, "Oh my, he has a very important message for you." Okay, here we go again, I thought, figuring I'd keep my intense interest to myself. I was already planning to give this one some serious tests once again.

Without my even turning her way, still measuring leather, she continued, "There is a little baby girl who is going to come to you when she is old enough, and you need to open your heart to her completely." She repeated herself exactly as the others had, "You must open your heart to her completely and teach her everything you know. This little girl has a very important job to do in the world and you need to teach her everything you know to help her achieve her purpose." Wow, could it have been any more spot on? Nope, it was the exact same message, almost word for word, except for one little thing. So, it was time for my testing to begin.

The first thing I asked her, as I continued measuring, was if the baby was still in the womb. She was surprised by my question, as she checked for an answer, "Oh wow, no, but she is just barely born only a couple weeks ago." In case you are wondering, I did the math, and sure enough, it was about 10 months since the psychic lady first told me this same message, when remember, the fetus was so young the mother may not have even known she was pregnant. Even without the math, that was an interesting response, and I realized later, it even gave me an approximate date for this girl's birthday, a sure fire way of identifying the right girl.

Then, of course, it was time for the next test question, "how important is this job she's supposed to do?" "Oh, it's real important" "As important as, say, a messiah?" "Wow, I don't know if it is that important... (she was checking her sources again) well, actually, yes, it is that important", surprised by her own response. Realizing how profound that statement was, she changed it a bit to, "or at least it is along those same lines of the type of job she has to do for the world, it's very important".

She had my attention now, since I was done measuring, so it was time for the final test question, the obvious one, "Do I know the mother?" She said without hesitation, "You don't know her now, but you will meet her shortly after you return to America". That's when she realized, "Oh wow, you're getting ready to return to America soon, aren't you. I'd better buy everything I need now, before you close the shop.... No, you won't be leaving until after January so I still have time to come back".

That did it, I was convinced this time, because I had never told ANYONE that we were getting ready to close the store and move back to America. In fact, we were planning to close the shop within about 10 days, so she wouldn't be

Finding Purpose

able to come back, but we weren't going to head back to America until after January.

She was right about when we'd return to America, but wrong about when the store was to be closed only because of her own assumptions, and I wasn't about to let that secret out. I wanted to tell her, so I could sell her some more stuff, but I didn't dare say a word with my employee standing there listening to every word of this conversation. I was trying to remain true to my Guru's advice to keep my moving plans to myself, and it's a good thing I did.

That's my "messiah" story, as bizarre as it may seem. I don't know what that little girl is meant to do for the world, and I doubt if it is to become a full blown messiah, so don't get me wrong, I haven't lost my mind completely. I should add, however, I do now know the little girl's mother and have met this little girl, even though I've lost contact since meeting her several years ago. Also, the mother told me once, that she carried that baby girl a full 10 months, making the timing of the messages even more precise.

The point is, Spirit did choose me for a specific purpose, which for one thing, was to be a spiritual teacher for at least one little girl. All these years later, spiritual insight is all I could teach about, because it's all I care about. Besides, I haven't kept up the pace with all the computer changes, so it's really all I know in these latter years of my life.

So you see, even though I couldn't imagine what I could know enough to teach anyone way back then, much less teach a messiah, it exactly fits with what I know now all these years later. It also fits with that message, which I actually received 3 times as well, that I would be speaking on a worldwide stage discussing my "work". I didn't know what my "work" was back then, when I first received those messages, but I definitely know what it is now, since that is exactly how Spirit refers to my book with every communication I now have.

You see, all these years later, I also am now someone who is able to receive messages from Spirit. I know what it's like to be the channeler, which is closer to the real purpose of my psychic abilities rather than reading tarot cards. But again, more on that later.

Back To America

With all these subtle clues showing me my destiny, one after another, unsolicited and full of valid proofs, one thing was becoming clear to me. There must be a divine purpose for my life, and the sooner I accept that, the closer I will get to fulfilling my Grand Canyon promise and returning to that ecstasy of the spiritual realm. To this day I look forward to that. Since that information came to me while still within the all-knowingness, it is something I can be completely confident in.

It's actually a very hard thing to accept, that you have such a high calling, or that Spirit wants you to do such astounding things as teaching the next messiah or saving lost souls. I'm still having a problem with what or how I'm supposed to achieve any of it. But all these years later, I do know I have some serious spiritual insight I could teach to anyone who is open enough to listen.

I've always had a problem with low self-esteem, which made accepting my spiritual destiny even more difficult. But, by the time we were getting ready to return to America, enough bizarre things had happened that I had to accept that these things were happening to me for a reason. People just don't normally have these kinds of spiritual experiences happen to them in their lives, especially as many times as they've happened to me, and without even seeking out divine inspiration.

We'd been in Australia nearly 8 years, and 5 of them were full of one spiritual phenomenon after another. Most of them were too subtle or irrelevant to mention here, such as the prediction from my Guru surrounding our move. But, they included some astounding manifestations, like when I actually watched a man transform into an Indian right in front of my eyes, and a Guru performing a miracle for me, and a set of 3 identical messages from complete strangers.

Then there were also those profound encounters that happened before our move to Australia. I can't forget my angel's message or the overpowering Joy, Love and all-knowing wisdom I experienced at the Grand Canyon. Who has this many overwhelming spiritual experiences happen to them in a lifetime? There had to be some purpose behind it, and I needed to recognize that this was really happening to me for a reason. The day finally came, when I felt I had to accept my calling.

It was soon after we had decided to return to America, and shortly after I'd had my numerology chart done, which was also very eye opening, when I sat down alone with Spirit and prayed for the first time in decades. It was the day I turned my life over to Spirit. I made a vow that day, with all my heart and soul and mind, to do whatever Spirit wanted me to do. I swore to follow whatever leads he sent me, to pay attention to whatever signs I was given, and do my very best to fulfill whatever he has in mind for me. I had no idea where it would lead me, but I meant it with everything I had. In my mind, my life was no longer my own.

Seeking My Destiny

Once I'd turned my life over to Spirit, I spent every waking moment keeping an eye out for spiritual signs, and was virtually in a constant state of prayer. Now that I'd finally accepted that Spirit had some specific purpose in mind for me, I wanted to get on with it. I prayed for guidance, even stumbling through Indian-like ceremonial prayers, not really knowing what I was doing. I was trying to stress my pure intentions so I could get started with my spiritual destiny. I did everything I could think of to get started on my path, but nothing came in the form of answers.

By now, we were back in America living on a beautiful 6 acre property we'd purchased with 2 spring fed ponds, but with only a single wide mobile home to reside in. It was a fair distance out in the country, far from any town, with the closest convenience store more than 10 miles away. We loved that property, though, and I felt very close to Spirit there. Right away, I started to get a strange image of several tents and some teepees in our yard that stuck with me like a sore tooth. I didn't know what it meant or what to do with it, so I just let it go as being strange mind chatter.

To stay busy, I relaunched my craft business as an internet only enterprise this time. It was 1999 by now and the internet was starting to get some attention by shoppers. Turns out, my computer programming background came in handy when it came time to develop a web site. The interesting thing, is now my website was beginning to attract spiritual people to me even in America.

A Spiritual Lady

One was a spiritual lady, whom I grew very close to via numerous phone conversations and emails. To this day, I've never met her in person, because she lives far away on the east coast somewhere. She was very spiritually inclined, but when I first met her, she was a newbie on her spiritual journey as well.

She had a very disabling illness, and was taking so many prescription drugs it was ridiculous, dozens of pills daily. She was determined to take herself off all the drugs with the help of Spirit, even though her doctors were saying it would kill her. Her attitude was that she would rather die than keep on living with the side effects of all those drugs. She knew in her heart that the doctors were wrong, that she could live through it with time.

I supported her efforts as much as I could over the phone, and she was making excellent strides towards getting off the drugs. Her doctors were shocked by her progress, and she wasn't even telling them how many of the drugs she'd stopped taking, at least not until she was sure she could get along without them. By the time we'd gone our separate ways, she was down to only about a 1/2 dozen drugs per day, but they were going to be the hardest to put behind her. She would have to cure herself from her illness to achieve it.

Just so you know, I contacted that lady several years later, and she not only had completely cured herself of her disease, and had been completely off all drugs for years, but she told me she had become an Indian shaman. The way I see it, is she came briefly into my life to introduce me to something I now know I needed to help me along on my spiritual journey. I'll get to that in a minute, but first let me tell you about a dream she had about me.

Vision Of Truth

    She said she saw me on my property, where she saw some buildings, including a barn, and some tents and teepees in my back yard. I was shocked and delighted when she told me of this, since this description exactly matches that strange image of tents and teepees that still continues to pop up in my head, even to this day. She had no knowledge of my own thoughts on this topic, so again, Spirit is providing me evidence of what could still be coming.

    We had a single barn on that 6 acre property, but we also have a barn on the property I now live on, as well as some additional buildings. Also remember the psychic lady's vision, where she saw a ceremony going on among a bunch of tents and teepees with fires in front of them. Truth is, I'd forgotten that the vision from my psychic lady included tents and teepees, and how it also matched this image of my land I was regularly having, until I sat down to write this book. Writing this really is helping me put the jigsaw puzzle together.

A Channeled Spirit

    What that spiritual lady with the illness introduced me to was a book. She wanted me to tell her what I thought of it, since it spoke of healing yourself. The first chapter was available in full to read for free online, so I went to the site and what I found there astounded me. Not only did I feel it would help her, I knew absolutely, it was speaking the truth, because it spoke of something I felt no other human being on the planet knew except for myself. I even doubted the author of the book understood the words I'd just read. Because, you see, the book was a channeled book, where the author just put down words being channeled by a spiritual entity.

    Right there, in the very first chapter of this book were the words, "Love energy", two words that I had never seen put side by side anywhere in the physical realm prior to this. It also spoke briefly about what Love energy is, referring to it as the ultimate power available to mankind, but leaving out the details of Love energy I'm here to tell the world. This book was speaking MY TRUTH, what I'd been shown at the Grand Canyon to be the absolute reality of our universe.

I purchased it on the spot, and even ordered the 2nd and 3rd books right away. There have now been 13 books published of the same type, and another 5 or 6 written without being completely channeled information. The interesting part of this is in all those 13 channeled books, of which I've read in full, there was never another mention of Love energy, as if that information is still being reserved for me to share with the world. It's as if he'd touched on the topic just enough to attract me specifically to his teachings. It's the way Spirit works, you know, especially this Spirit, who calls himself Kryon.

Of course, I realize, there are going to be a lot of doubters out there reading this, because now we are talking about that weird thing called channeling. Well, I've had enough weird things happen to me to know that channeling is not even weird at all. Besides, I'm here to tell you my story, and Kryon has been a very big part of it, so doubt all you want. Remember, I'm a skeptic too, so I get it. But, I was shown as absolute that Kryon speaks the truth and in many more ways than just that small paragraph in the first chapter of his first channeled book. He has given numerous predictions, all of which have come true, surrounding science and the direction humanity was taking and has taken.

The thing that kills me about people who doubt the process called channeling, is they are usually Christians even though the Bible is full of channeled information. What are they thinking? Do they think God just abandoned us humans once the Bible was written, never to converse with another human being ever again? Of course, God hasn't abandoned us, and his method of communication with humanity hasn't changed either. He continues to channel information through the mind of man, which is exactly what that scary thing they fear so much, called "channeling", is.

Oh, but that was different back then in biblical days, because that was God speaking, and this is some spooky thing called a "spirit". What a joke! God is a Spirit, after all, which is an exact quote from the Bible (*"God is a Spirit"*, John 4:24.). In fact, something that really surprised me early on in his channels is when Kryon referred to himself as "I AM THAT I AM". He even said he is the same entity who spoke to Moses on the mountain. He tells us, that he is of the family of Michael the Archangel, and that "Kryon" is not his actual name, but is the closest he can get to the sound his energy makes from within the spiritual realm.

Enough said on this. I'm not going to continue trying to convince you of anything I believe. You can take it or leave it, as your journey dictates. I'm just here to tell you my story, and as one skeptic to another, I was given the proof I needed to open my mind to the many teachings this entity has shared with mankind. If you are willing to open your mind, you could surely learn something from him as well. You can find his website at www.kryon.com if interested. I've included this link in the references section as well.

Anyway, at this point, it was just some books I was reading. There were some fascinating teachings there, but nothing beyond the realm of realistic possibility. Kryon teaches very slowly, just as Spirit teaches slowly, so this was simply an easy way for Spirit to get me educated on the way things are, as I adjusted slowly to the realization of what it means to be a human being.

Self-healing is only one example of that, which is what my spiritual lady friend was able to gain enough confidence in to achieve, thanks to those books from Kryon. Just so you know, his messages are filled with Love and compassion designed to help mankind through the evolutionary step we are currently taking. We will discuss Kryon some more in the chapters to come, since he became a very important part of my life later on.

My Indian Grandmother

I was starting to learn some important spiritual truths, thanks to those Kryon books, and I was still very much into my Indian heritage, wanting to learn all I could about it as well. As I waited patiently for the next Kryon book to be published, I tried to study up further on animal totems, and continued to pray for my spiritual journey to begin. Clearly, it had begun, but it was only a slow process of learning, and I wanted to be helpful to someone somehow.

Actually, that also was happening, since the spiritual lady was still getting my support through the phone for her self-healing, and I was also publishing a newsletter through my website which was helping a lot of people in a lot of ways I was barely aware of. It's just that those things were so easy and came so naturally, that I didn't feel like I was doing anything in answer to my spiritual calling. The point is, sometimes we are doing exactly what we are meant to be doing even as we eagerly seek more meaning in life. The meaning we seek is often in the small things.

This is about when another spiritual lady managed to find me through my website, an Indian elder. She wasn't specific on what she wanted from me, but had noticed that we didn't live that far apart, so she asked, via email, if I would come to see her. I was so excited, feeling sure that it must have been Spirit sending her in answer to my prayers. Her actual goal was to see if I would sell her finished goods on my website, but I didn't know that. I was thinking she was just a lady who wanted some company, and I was definitely willing to do that, especially since I was hoping to find an Indian mentor at the time.

When I went to visit her the first time, I did my best to approach her in the right way, the Indian way, with the plan to ask her to be my teacher. I brought her some tobacco and some sage as gifts, and nervously told her what my hopes were. She laughed, and told me she normally would have declined, but because I'd done my best to request her mentoring the respectful way, she would think about it, but definitely not until I had done it correctly. She told me how I should have done it, and also to go home and think about it first, because it wasn't something I should take so lightly, without even knowing her first.

Then she told me what she actually wanted, for me to sell her goods online, and I was glad to do that for her. In the end, she not only became my mentor, but she adopted me in the "Indian way", which is why I refer to her as my Indian Grandmother. Just understand, we weren't actually related by blood, only by Spirit, even though she looked so much like me it was astounding. And by the way, she was Cherokee.

I would go to visit my Indian Grandmother on a weekly basis, sometimes twice a week, even though she lived about an hour's drive from my house. Among the things my Indian Grandmother taught me, was how to sacrifice something to receive what you seek, such as when you plant sage. She always returned some of the crop to the earth in appreciation for the gift it was giving her. She also showed me the proper way to hold a personal prayer ceremony as a way to send a very important message to Spirit, and how to open my heart and quiet my mind to listen to Spirit.

She told me meditation is not necessary for speaking with Spirit, which was a huge relief to me, since meditation is not my thing. I've tried it, but it bores me, and it's not long before I'm ready to end it. I always thought that was something I was going to have to get beyond if I was ever going to be spiritual. Turns out, you don't ever have to meditate to be spiritual if you don't want to. At least not in the normal ways people do meditation.

She was very connected to Spirit, and on occasion, she would tell me a message Spirit was sending her to tell me. One of those messages, interestingly enough, was that she could see tents and teepees in my back yard. She said the tents would be used for sleeping and the teepees would be used for ceremonies. I was so excited to hear this, since it was another confirmation that my own images had meaning, even though I still didn't know what the meaning was.

Now that I'm reviewing this for this book, I have to point out once again; I was sent 3 confirmations of those images of tents and teepees in my back yard. First, the psychic lady in Australia, then the spiritual lady who healed herself, and finally my Indian Grandmother. Clearly, the potential is there for tents and teepees to be erected in my back yard, but to date, that time has not yet come. There is still more to come that could indicate what these tents and teepees are going to be for, but for chronological reasons, we will get to that later in this chapter.

Another one of those random messages she would get from Spirit to tell me, was that she could see the land I would spend the rest of my life on. She said the property she saw me living on for the remainder of my days had a single pond with grass growing right up to the water. She also said it had a small berm of land raising up to hold the water in.

We were actually looking for a new house to live in temporarily at the time. That single wide mobile home was just too small for my growing business, so we were planning on finding a house to live in long enough to establish the business better, and then build a house near 1 of the 2 ponds on our property, while renting out the single wide mobile. We found a pretty nice house on 5+ acres with a pond and several outbuildings. The pond was way in the back of the property, however, so I never really inspected it, since it was too far away to get any enjoyment out of anyway. Besides, this was a temporary residence, in our minds, so it didn't matter what the pond looked like.

That all changed, however, when a man came asking if he could buy the land behind our house, since it is on a corner and the back of this new property is easily accessible from the road. We thought that would be a good way to get a down payment for the house we were going to build, so we were glad to sell it. We set out doing the survey required to divide the land and refinanced it so the back part was excluded from our mortgage, leaving half of our land now free and clear, ready to sell. Problem is, when we called the man to tell him it was ready for him to buy, he sadly informed us that he was about to get laid off from his work, so he was no longer able to buy anything.

Finding Purpose

In all of our looking around for options of getting a larger residence, we'd spent a lot of time looking at double-wide mobile homes, and learned about how you can get a very reasonable price if you buy one in the process of foreclosure. It was my idea that we go ahead and get one of those foreclosed homes for this land we now have free and clear, since with a residence on it, the property would sell for heaps more. There was some real profit to be made on this deal, but we had to live in the new residence to get a loan approved.

That is how it happened, all completely by accident, or should I say, by divine intervention. Not only was the nearly new double-wide mobile we ended up getting sight unseen an excellent buy, but it turned out to be a completely upgraded home, with things like double thick walls, plywood floors and oak cabinets. We fell in love with this property during those years we had to live here, and even lost our desire to build a new house elsewhere.

The astounding thing is, we'd lived on this property nearly 3 years before we discovered that the pond was exactly as my Indian Grandmother had described. She was right too; this is where I plan to spend the rest of my days, on this peaceful 5+ acre property backed by a ravine, which will keep encroaching neighbors from building anything behind us. The new home is located very near the large pond, where the grass grows all the way to the water, making it an easy stroll to go enjoy it.

My time with my Indian Grandmother covered about a three year period, when she died unexpectedly. She had become my confidant, the only person I could come to regarding spiritual matters, so her passing was a huge loss to me. Many other things were going on during those three years, most of which I also plan to tell you about, since they were filled with Spirit. But, trying to keep this in chronological order is getting difficult, since all kinds of things were happening and are therefore overlapping each other. The only way to move forward is by backing up to describe the various things happening simultaneously.

Eagle Awareness

The fascinating thing about this next experience is I'd filed it away in my memory as something that happened in Australia. But just now, as I started to write this story down, I realized it wasn't in Australia, because the bedroom I woke up in wasn't in any house we'd lived in there. I just realized it was on THIS property, in the bedroom of the house we first lived in here, which is now a rental house. Once again, writing this all down is really helping me sort it all out.

It is VERY significant and an exciting revelation for me, that it happened where I now live, but to explain why, I need to describe the experience first. It started with a dream about a ceremony or even several ceremonies, but I don't remember the specifics of the dream itself. What I do remember as clearly as if it happened yesterday, is I suddenly woke up and sat straight up in my bed.

I was wide awake, and in my mind I was receiving a VERY clear message, where Spirit was telling me how extremely important it was that I remember this. It wasn't the dream itself that was important, but what was generally going on in the dream and that I needed to call **IT** the Eagle Awareness Program. It was soooo crucial to Spirit that I remember that name, so I promised Spirit I would brand that name into my memory, even though I had no idea why. Obviously, I've made good on that promise, since I will never forget that title to who knows what.

Finding Purpose

First of all, what does it even mean, a "program"? I wondered what would be required for something to be considered a "program". And then there is the obvious question of why "Eagle Awareness"? What is that supposed to be representing? I had no idea why it was so important to remember this, or what "program" Spirit was referring to. All I knew is Spirit was telling me to be sure to remember this title, and as the servant to Spirit I was, it wasn't my job to question what I am being asked to do.

All these years later, more has happened to help me understand what the title does represent. Even though I still don't know what the "program" might look like in the end, something is beginning to develop in my mind. It is just so far from a reality that I can't even begin to establish a plan for it to materialize. However, I do know where to get my hands on a teepee of any size thanks to my Indian craft supply business.

As far as the title of "Eagle Awareness" is concerned, you should understand first that the eagle is my Indian totem. I know this from a sequence of dreams literally designed to teach me about my totem and also that I can count on them to always be there for me. I say "them", because in the dreams there were 2 eagles, one a bald eagle and one a golden eagle. It's kind of funny, but the bald eagle was named Charlie Daniels and the golden eagle was called Jack Daniels. Believe me; I can't make this stuff up. An old rock and roll star and a type of whiskey, really? Both of them having the same last name was indicating to me that they were brothers.

The 2 eagles would sit on my shoulders as I went about doing normal life things. I remember in one dream, the last one I had, Jack was off doing something, so Charlie was the only eagle with me. When I bent down to get into a taxi, Charlie had to fly off my shoulder because he couldn't fit in the door. I got all upset and started crying because both of my eagles had left me. Suddenly both Charlie and Jack appeared there with me in the taxi. Charlie told me to never worry about them ever leaving my side, because even if it appeared they were gone, they were always with me and I could call on them at any time.

An Indian totem is the one animal that carries the energy closest to the energy you were born with, so in that way, it is your companion through life. The significance of the eagle is that it is the one bird that flies higher than any other bird, so it can see the big picture like no other animal on earth. It is also the animal signifying the eastern side of an Indian Medicine Wheel, which is the direction where "illumination" is represented. The big picture of the reality of mankind is what I was shown in my Grand Canyon experience, so it definitely does fit with my life energy, that an eagle would be my totem.

That's why this book series is called the Eagle Awareness Series, because its primary purpose is to teach the big picture of mankind's existence. Likewise, whatever this "program" is meant to be, if it ever materializes, it will also be called the "Eagle Awareness Program". Anything I would put together as a method of teaching would definitely be designed to teach the big picture of our human existence, so the title fits perfectly. I don't know why a title would be considered that important to Spirit, but I can say that having that name anchored in my mind has led me down some paths I am still following even as I write this.

Realizing now, that I had that dream when we first moved to this property, is very significant, because it is a confirmation that what I have been getting haunted by in my thoughts for more than a decade now, the image of

Finding Purpose

tents and teepees in my yard, is something I am meant to do on THIS land. In fact, I've been getting a strong desire to establish a spiritual retreat on this beautiful property lately. Problem is, however, it is a huge undertaking, so I would need help, initially making it just a pipe dream. If you are interested in the progress of this "program", you can go to my website, www.eagle-awareness.com, to find an update. I could really use feedback from people to see if there is any interest in a spiritual retreat. Come find me and tell me what you'd like to see included in the "program".

Destiny On Track

When we first moved into our 3 bedroom house on the property with 1 pond, where I still live in a double-wide mobile behind the house, I started to get another strange thought. This was very much like the thought of tents and teepees, except I didn't like this thought, because it wasn't my thing. I've always enjoyed camping, so tents were okay with me, and my Indian heritage made the teepees appealing as well. But this uninvited thought was not something I had any interest in, writing a book.

Whatever I would be doing, the thought would come up to write a book about it, which was just out of the question. When I was trying a new diet of my own design, for example, the thought would come to write a diet book. Once while watching our new president on television, I remember thinking I should write a book on politics. I'd catch myself having these strange thoughts, and be like "What? Me write a book on politics? That's just nuts!" Not only am I not about to write any book, but to even begin the extensive research required to write one on politics was far beyond something I would ever consider doing. Why in the world would I even think of such a thing? Where are these thoughts coming from? It was annoying, because they were simply not thoughts I would normally have.

It never even occurred to me, that they were messages from Spirit. I was still too much of an infant regarding spiritual communication. I just kept getting repeatedly annoyed by them, and threw them away as being ridiculous mind chatter every time they came up. Eventually, Spirit made it clear where the thoughts of writing books were coming from and why, but that is another one of those stories that are coming up soon. I'm trying to stay as close to chronological order as possible, and Spirit always made me wait years before the clarity would come, so chronologically speaking, you will have to wait too.

Experiencing Kryon

While still living in what is now the rental house on this property, there were several things that happened surrounding Kryon, the Spirit who is channeling all those books I was still reading. I'm going to tell you some of the things concerning Kryon to help you get to know this spiritual entity and just how powerful his presence can be.

The more I read the books of Kryon, the more I wanted to know about his channeler, Lee Carroll. Lee's story is short and sweet, because he really doesn't talk much about himself. From what I understand, before Kryon started sending him messages, he was a devout Baptist working as an engineer, the last kind of person you would expect would become a spiritual channeler.

He said it all started with him getting messages usually while he was taking a shower. He would receive these strong messages in his mind, which he tried to ignore and fight off at first. He was being told, by Kryon, to share

Destiny On Track

the information Kryon was giving him, but he insisted on proof before he would tell a soul what was happening to him.

Since he was a scientist by nature, science was the only real proof he could accept, so Kryon gave him several scientific predictions. Over the next 2 years, all those predictions came true, so Lee had to finally acknowledge that the phenomenon happening to him must be legitimate. He finally agreed to share it with a few people, some of his closest friends, and hence, he did his first channeling in public.

I wanted to witness this channeling process first hand myself, so I went to a couple of his "At Home" meetings, which are very small informal gatherings of about 50-80 people. Everyone attending pays a small fee, and he comes to channel Kryon live, as well as let you know about the most recent predictions Kryon had presented in prior channels, all of which have come true by then. Lee actually channels Kryon all over the world to very large audiences these days, and has been for about 25 years or so now. The United Nations has even invited him to speak on several occasions. So these small "At Home" meetings are a very intimate and special experience, and illustrate Lee's dedication to getting the word out to anyone willing to listen.

The first "At Home" meeting I went to was just across the border in Arkansas, a short 3 hour drive from where I live. The strangest thing happened upon my arrival. I had just paid my money at the little table outside the hotel banquet room, when I noticed Lee coming down the hall towards the entry. I'm not really sure how I knew it was him, I just knew. The strange thing was I felt a VERY strong sense of recognition coming from Lee towards me. It was like he knew me really well, and it seemed like he was even hurrying to reach me before I went into the room so he could greet me.

The feeling of recognition was so strong, that to be polite, I thought I should wait for him. I know this sounds strange, because I had never met this person in my life, and yet it was very clear to me that he knew me, or at least thought he did. I was anxious to learn how he thought he knew me.

The strangest part about it, is the closer he got to me, the more the feeling of recognition dissipated. By the time he reached the sign in table, where I stood nearby, the feeling of recognition was completely gone. He never even glanced my way, except to give me a shy smile as he entered the room like anyone would towards someone staring at them. I was actually embarrassed that I'd waited on him for what seemed like several minutes. I wanted to approach him and tell him why I'd been staring at him all this time. But, I was also shy and just fell in line with the rest of the guests to hear the live channeling.

The meeting itself was an interesting experience, but it was that recognition thing that I will never forget. The next day, I went to visit a friend of mine to tell her all about the meeting, since I'd told her about Kryon and the many books I'd read of his channels. She was a local psychic I was friends with for a while, but I haven't seen her for years now. On this day, however, she had a revelation as I was telling her this recognition story. She said, "Kathy, it wasn't Lee who was recognizing you, it was Kryon!!" Of course, that was the only thing that made sense.

Kryon has often said that he knows us all very well from the other side of the veil. It fits exactly with the fact that the recognition went away the closer the human being,

Lee, got to me. I was feeling the recognition from the entity that was constantly with Lee, from Kryon, until the human in control came close enough for me to feel his energy instead of Kryon's. That was my first spiritual experience surrounding Kryon, or should I call it, spiritual sensation, but it was far from my last.

My First Cyndy Party

That same friend, the local psychic, invited me to what she called a "Cyndy Party" one day. It's basically a spiritual twist to the Tupperware party, where people gather together to ask a psychic lady named Cyndy questions for a small fee. It turns out; Cyndy is very good at what she does. I was astounded at some of the precise answers people were getting and the reaction it was causing among the small group.

Cyndy went through a ritual of preparing herself, which included double blind folding herself. Everyone would write down their question on a small piece of paper. With the papers gathered together in a box, Cyndy would hold them up to her head, one after another, until one of them would give her a clear message. She would then call on the person the message was for and proceed to answer their question with extensive details.

My question was about a spiritual retreat I'd heard about, a 3-day event in a remote town west of Denver. It boasted that Lee Carroll was supposed to attend for daily Kryon channels. Even though it wasn't hosted by Lee Carroll, it was based on the Kryon teachings. I wanted to know if it was something Spirit thought I could benefit from.

I'd never been to any spiritual retreat before, so I had no idea what it would entail, and it wouldn't be a cheap journey. Even though the retreat itself was very reasonably priced at less than $400 including 2 meals per day, the hotel where it was being held was a 5 star hotel. So, this was 3 days at a 5 star hotel plus the travel expense of getting there plus the $400. I thought it sounded like it would be interesting, but I didn't want to waste my money if it wasn't really something Spirit wanted me to do.

The thing that made this experience interesting was how Cyndy told us to address our questions. She said we could address it to someone we love who passed away, or to someone we look up to, like Jesus, or any other Spirit we may want to come answer our question for us. Since Kryon has often said in his channels, that anyone of us can call on him whenever we want and he will come to us, I went ahead and addressed my question to Kryon. This is when I first learned just how intense the experience of having Kryon come to you truly is.

The first thing that happened, when Cyndy came upon my piece of paper, was a long pause as she gathered herself due to the intense vibration she was experiencing. None of us knew what the delay was, but then that intensity started to come over me. It felt like a vibration going through my entire body, and it became so intense, that I went into a sort of trance like state, even though I was still fully aware of what was going on around me. Cyndy started to describe what she was seeing, which was an unusual way for her to try to find the person this message was for. She said she was seeing a deep purple color and a gold crown. Then finally she saw the letter "K". Because of the vibrations I was feeling, and because both Kryon and my own name starts with a "K", I knew this message was for me.

I don't remember her exact words, but she said there was some class or classes she saw coming up. I knew right away, she was referring to the spiritual retreat I'd asked about. She told me it would be a good class for me to attend, that I would learn a lot. She said that the entire experience would help me towards my purpose in life, or something like that.

There was actually a lot to my message, because I'd cheated and asked 3 questions instead of the 1 question we were supposed to ask on my piece of paper. I figured I would only receive one answer, but thought I'd ask 3 questions just to insure I got an answer to something I wanted to know. In fact, all three questions were answered very clearly, so my message was much longer than the norm, which meant the vibrational trance I was experiencing also went on for quite a while. Cyndy also experienced the intense vibration throughout the process, evidenced by her comment on how powerful that entity was when it was over.

I have to say, even though each time Kryon has shown up in my life the sensation has been somewhat different, Kryon WILL be heard, that's for sure. He definitely is a very powerful entity, where you are left with no doubt that you were visited by a spiritual force. Also, showing Cyndy the deep purple color with the gold crown did serve a purpose which came up later, so watch for it.

Journey To The Retreat

Needless to say, I signed up to go to the spiritual retreat and started to prepare for my journey. Due to my disability, traveling alone for the 8+ hour drive was going to be difficult, so I decided to stop half way there to lessen the strain on me. After spending so much money on the retreat, however, I didn't want to add to the expense by staying in another hotel or even cheap motel.

Since I would be driving my conversion van, which has a double bed in the back, I decided I would just sleep over in a rest area. I located one on the map in Kansas just outside the Colorado border, which was nearly half the distance to the retreat location. I arrived at the rest area just before dark on this mid-April day in 2001.

I've noticed that, for some unknown reason, major changes in my life, good or bad, seem to be marked by the month of April. It's the month when the Angel spoke to me and 20 years later when my wakeup call happened. It's when we arrived in Australia and back home in America, when this retreat took place, and it's even the month when my husband died. It's been so prevalent, that I've started to pay attention to what happens in April, even though it's usually an uneventful month.

Anyway, I settled in for the night in the back of my van at my chosen rest area, and decided to hold my own little ceremonial prayer in preparation for this spiritual retreat I was about to attend. I got out my personal Indian pipe; hand carved with an eagle head bowl, along with my sage and kinnick-kinnick (Indian tobacco) and carefully followed the steps my Indian Grandmother had taught me on how to hold a very serious prayer. I was praying for my fears to be transformed into Love, and for my heart to remain open to whatever I was meant to learn at this retreat.

I remember receiving a message in my thoughts from Spirit that night, telling me I should tell someone at the retreat about my experience at the Grand Canyon. Receiving messages myself was something I still wasn't used to yet, so I wondered why I was having that thought, again assuming it was something I was thinking rather than a message from Spirit. I figured it was about time I did tell someone though, and decided I would tell Lee, since he was the only one I knew who was going to be at the retreat, even though he didn't really know me.

As I was finishing up my ceremony, I noticed it was starting to sprinkle some rain outside my van, and the wind was picking up substantially. So, I added a small prayer to my ceremony, asking Spirit to keep me safe from the weather for the night. Feeling confident that my prayers would be answered, I put my ceremonial items away and cuddled up to sleep for the night.

When I had to go to the public restroom during the night, I remember having no problem avoiding the occasional sprinkles of light rain and the wind wasn't blowing as severely as it was earlier. Reassured, that Spirit was taking care of me by keeping the weather mild, I climbed back in the van to sleep soundly the rest of the night. I awoke very early in the morning, since I'd gone to sleep just after dark, to dry sidewalks and the sun shining brightly. The rest area was now full of semi-trucks and other travelers. I was the first among them to head out to continue my journey.

I'd only gone a few miles down the road when I was startled to notice some traces of snow along the sides of the road. This was mid-April, remember, so the last thing I expected to run into was snow. I'd only gone 7 miles down the road from the rest area, with the snow becoming more and more prevalent with every mile, when I came across a road block stopping me dead in my tracks.

I was shocked by the sight ahead of me, the interstate solid white with snow and ice at least 2 feet deep at its lowest point with snow drifts reaching 7-8 feet high towering far above the guard rails. There was so much snow and ice, that it was clear, no traffic had driven on that road ahead in many hours. The sign at the road block ahead confirmed this, since it was announcing to me in bold letters, the ROAD IS CLOSED!!

With no other options available to me, I proceeded down the exit indicated and found myself in a small off road area where the only buildings were a couple motels, a gas station, and a small coffee shop. I needed some breakfast anyway, so I went to the coffee shop, where I found a parking lot almost completely full of semi-trucks. The coffee shop was brimming with activity, making me consider myself lucky to find a tiny table right next to the kitchen.

Once settled in, I turned my attention to all the chatter going on between the many truckers waiting for the road to open. They were discussing their options, such as taking the exit road itself straight into the next town and then over to meet the highway above the storm. Others were saying that wouldn't work, since some had already tried it, and had to turn back because that road was too hard to travel. Someone else told the room, that the news is saying the highway is closed all the way to Wyoming.

Then a lady trucker came in and joined some trucker friends of hers at one of the tables. She had a loud voice, and was virtually talking to everyone in the room anyway, as she proceeded to exclaim her relief to be alive. She said she had gone through a tornado the night before, and the truck directly in front of her was picked up by the wind and thrown off the road to be laid on its side. She said, all she could do is pull over and wait for the twister to pass her by, since her truck was about to join it.

I was astonished by what I was hearing from these people who had weathered a huge storm I could only see evidence of from the resulting snow everywhere. No wonder the snow drifts were so high, I thought to myself, as I strained my ears to take all this in. Nobody seemed to know when the roads would be opened again, but it didn't look good.

After finishing my breakfast, I headed over to the biggest of the motels, where there was a large lobby with a TV set tuned into the weather channel. It was then, that I realized how profoundly secure my little ceremonial prayer had made me. There on the screen was a map of the storm with the areas hit indicated in white. Just outside the Colorado border of this map, in Kansas right on the highway where I'd stayed for the night in that little rest area, was a perfect circle NOT colored in white. I had been completely surrounded by massive blizzards and even tornados all night, and yet all I experienced in my safe little circle was a sprinkle of rain and some wind.

I watched in disbelief as the newscaster described this record breaking storm that covered 3 states, reaching all the way to Illinois. They were saying all the roads were closed, and would be for a while, so I knew I had a serious wait on my hands. It was now unseasonably cold outside, so staying in my van wasn't a good idea anymore. I considered myself extremely lucky to get one of the last rooms available in the smaller of the 2 motels. Spirit was still taking care of me, I thought.

It was still early in the day, so I killed some time watching TV in my room, while I repeatedly called the phone number I'd found to check the status of the road conditions. I was determined to stay up through the night so I could hit the road as soon as they opened. As the day turned to night, my plan to stay at the retreat hotel for the night was becoming an obvious impossibility, even though I was only about 4 hours away from my destination, that is,

Vision Of Truth

in good driving conditions. I was losing hope of making it to the retreat at all, and thought this trip must not be in the cards.

The thing that had me really worried was facing the drive ahead in the snow, even if the roads did open. My only experience driving in an area where it snowed was our brief life in Montana, where I'd had 2 horrible accidents resulting from the snow and ice. I'd turned the age of driving while living in Florida, then moved to Arizona where I met my husband, then to Montana for a few years, and then Seattle where again, it never snows. Then there was Australia, where it also never snows, and finally Oklahoma has very little snow as well. I am very inexperienced at driving in snow, plus I was driving a top heavy van with normal tires and no load in the back to keep me grounded.

Finally, by about midnight, I was feeling like this trip was not meant to be, but was confused by the conflicting message I'd received at the Cyndy party. I decided it was time to pray again. After figuring out the latest possible time the road could open for me to make it to my destination before the proceedings began the next morning, I started my prayer to Spirit. I told Spirit that the road would have to open by 1AM, or 2AM at the very latest, so if Spirit wants me to go to that retreat, he'd better make sure the road was open by then. I swore to Spirit, that I refuse to show up at the retreat late, so if the roads aren't open by then, I was going home.

With my ultimatum clearly stated, being the demanding servant I can be sometimes, I decided I should try to grab a nap. I prayed to Spirit to please awaken me if the roads opened in time, not having too much hope that they would. It was about an hour later, when I found myself suddenly awake, feeling panicked that I'd slept through the night. I realized it was only 1:30AM, so I immediately called for the road condition status. Sure enough, the road was open and I was checked out and on the road by 2 am, right on time. Clearly, Spirit wanted me to attend this retreat, so I was going to do my absolute best to overcome my fears of driving in the snow.

The snow plows had done their job well on this interstate, but the effects of the storm were more and more obvious the closer I got to Denver. It's not like the road had been traveled on much either, since I was one of the first to head out on the newly opened road, so prior tires weren't warming up the highway ahead of me. In a nutshell, I got more and more terrified the closer I got to Denver. By the time I got there, trying to drive as fast as I could dare, which was well under the normal pace an experienced driver would take, I was already a basket case.

I decided to make a quick pit stop when I spotted a Denny's Restaurant on the other side of Denver. I knew I had to hurry, because it was already 5am and the retreat was supposed to start in 3 hours, so I just grabbed some coffee and a donut and was on the road again by 5:30am. I thought I was closer than I was, because in miles I was less than half way, but in road conditions, not even close. From that point on, I had to leave the interstate to reach the remote town where this retreat was being held, which meant traveling through winding mountain roads and steep inclines both up and down.

I was already scared driving on the interstate, and now I'm traveling on a road where every moment was sheer terror. When I left Denny's, I had hopes of arriving in time to check in and grab a decent meal, but that dream was long gone, and now I was just hoping to arrive at all. Even though these roads usually had a speed limit of 50 or 60 mph, I was

Vision Of Truth

lucky to do 25 mph, and was often only going 10-15 mph. I mean, I was seriously scared for my life, with big semi-trucks or SUV's passing me in a vengeance spraying their road slush all over my windshield making matters worse.

Finally, I did arrive alive at my destination, but I was extremely exhausted to say the least. My hands had been so tightly clenched to the steering wheel for so long, that I had serious difficulty in wrenching them off of it. Then, just getting out of the van was a massive effort, walking with my cane made me feel in danger of falling, and I still had to climb a few stairs to get into this place. Checking in was all I could barely do, but trying to drag my luggage around with this exhausted body was out of the question, especially since it was already 8:30am and I was late. All I could manage was to find a place to sit down to begin some sort of recovery from that 6 hour drive of terror.

Thankfully, the retreat location in the hotel was right off the lobby, where I was really surprised to find hardly anybody there. Low and behold, everyone had trouble getting there due to the storm, with the airports shutting down and flights turned away. I'd never even thought of that possibility. The retreat was starting late, and I was actually a little early. I even had time to move my car to the proper parking garage and drag my bags up to my room. Still, there wasn't time to grab a meal, so my exhausted body wasn't getting the nutrients it needed to recover.

By the time the retreat broke for lunch, it had been over 30 hours since I'd had a proper breakfast in that coffee shop at the closed road exit, and I'd only gotten 1 hour of sleep, not to mention the incredibly stressful drive since then. They were taking only a 1/2 hour break to make up for some lost time, but I was still too exhausted to eat, and preferred to spend those precious moments relaxing somewhere with a cigarette. By the time the first day ended, which I was too tired to get much out of, all I wanted to do was find a bed.

Remembering the plan to tell Lee about my Grand Canyon experience, I stopped to tell him I wanted to talk to him as everyone was filing out of the retreat room. I was surprised, and in truth, put off a bit, when he told me it was Geoff I should speak to. Geoff was the one who had organized this event, but I didn't know him from Adam. I didn't want to approach a complete stranger with something as bizarre as my astounding spiritual experience.

Still embarrassed by the staring episode due to the recognition I felt at that "At Home" meeting, I thought Lee was looking at me as some kind of groupie or something, when nothing could be further from the truth. So, okay fine then, I wouldn't tell anyone about my Grand Canyon experience, so be it! I didn't know why I was suddenly going to tell somebody about it anyway. I'd kept it to myself this long, so why start sharing now?

I realized later, and you will soon see why, that it was Kryon who was telling me to go speak to Geoff. I don't know if Lee realizes it or not, but I think sometimes it is Kryon speaking for him without his knowledge, which in this case, at least, was entirely appropriate. Or perhaps Lee was being told by Kryon to direct me to Geoff. I just wish he would have shared that with me if it is true, since I took it as if he wasn't interested in anything I might have to say. I felt insulted to say the least.

With the retreat meetings done for the day, sleep was the only thing I cared about. As everyone else headed for the dining room, I went straight for the elevators to go to my room, where I met another lady from the retreat in the elevator bringing her luggage up. She told me her name and room number, and mentioned she was a psychic during the short elevator ride. I was so completely spent, that I hit the sack immediately upon throwing off my dirty clothes without even replacing them with sleep attire. They were the same clothes I'd worn from the start of this journey, so I just wanted to be free of my own filth and going commando was better than sleeping in dirty clothes. I wasn't in bed longer than a minute before I was sound asleep.

Spirits In My Room
　　The first day of the retreat had ended at about 7:30pm, and I was sound asleep by 7:40pm. But, even as exhausted as I was, that badly needed rest was short lived. It was only about 3 hours later when I started getting bothered by spirits waking me up, and I mean spirits were shouting at me! I was having another awesome spiritual experience, but I was in no shape to appreciate it. I woke up hearing all kinds of spirits bothering me, not letting me sleep, telling me I had to do something, except I didn't care, I just wanted to sleep. I'd repeatedly wake up to the buzzing racket of spirits yelling at me, and in my anger over the intrusion, I would just demand they let me go back to sleep.

　　Remember this, we are the boss, and so the spirits did obey my demand. Problem is, they quieted down only long enough for me to go back to sleep, and then they would wake me up again and again. That is, after all, exactly what I'd demanded of them, to let me go back to sleep. I never thought to add the request that they allow me to stay asleep. This is one way I learned how precise you need to be with your requests from Spirit.

This invasive interruption of my sleep went on for several hours, until finally, at 4am, I sat straight up in my bed, too irritated and too wide awake to fight them off any longer. I shouted at the air in my dark room, "What do you want from me!?!" I was very angry at the constant disruption these unseen spirits were causing to my badly needed rest.

That's when I started to get a feel for the magnitude of this experience. It wasn't just a spirit or two in my room with me that night. It felt more like hundreds of spirits, way too many to even fit in the room, reaching far out into the hallway. I remembered, from the day before, the leaders of the retreat had told us not to be surprised if we had spirits visit us during the night. They'd said many spirits came to this retreat to be with us during this exciting event, so we should just know, we are not alone here. I guess there had been some strange occurrences happen at previous events, since this was the 7th such retreat they'd held.

As soon as I'd asked what the spirits wanted from me, the answers came in multitudes, from every direction. It was like every one of these spirits were yelling at me, hundreds of anxious spirits trying to send me the same message at the same time, but each with their own way of wording the same thing. It was like standing in the middle of a crowd with everyone yelling at the same time, trying to make out what they were trying to say. I was hearing varying messages, "it's like it was when Jesus was here", or "it's just like it was with Jesus", with an occasional "you have to tell them" and "you have to tell him" thrown in the mix once in a while.

This was making no sense to me whatsoever. All I could figure out, is I had to tell someone something, someone who is a "him". I had no idea who "them" could be referring to at the time, but to me, "him" must be Lee. But, that wasn't going to work either. Lee was looking at me as some lame groupie person and had already let me know, he didn't want to talk to me.

I didn't know what to do with this, all while these hundreds of spirits continued to shout their concerns at me repeatedly, "it's like it was when Jesus was here", or "it's just like it was with Jesus", or something similar. They were all expressing their concerns with such a desperate tone, like it was a real problem someone had to fix right now. Finally, I said out loud, "What do you want me to do about it?" That's when they stopped shouting simultaneously and I heard, as if from two spirits only, "you have to tell them" and "you have to tell him".

With that said, they went silent briefly, as if to allow me to gather my thoughts for a moment. This is when I remembered the lady I'd met in the elevator. As soon as that thought came to mind, they started shouting their desperate pleas again, "it's like it was when Jesus was here", "it's just like it was with Jesus", "you have to tell them", and "you have to tell him".

It was very clear, they were extremely anxious for me to do something about this Jesus problem, whatever that was. It was as if they expected me to do something about it right there and then, at this very moment. It was 4 AM in the morning, for Pete's sake! This was insane, and I still badly needed some sleep.

The only thing I could think of, as the spirits continued shouting at me, was to call that psychic lady I'd met in the elevator in hopes she could help me make some sense of it all. But, I wasn't about to do that at 4 AM in the morning! Feeling pressured because these Spirits were so desperate, the only thing I thought of was that 6 AM wouldn't be nearly as bad as 4 AM to call that lady. So, I told the spirits, again out loud, that I would call her in the morning if they would let me sleep until "at least 6 AM". They immediately stopped their chatter, and I went quickly back to sleep.

In hindsight, I wished I'd have told them 7 AM rather than "at least" 6 AM, because they didn't hear the "at least" part. At EXACTLY 6 AM, I was awoken by all the spirits again, shouting simultaneously about this Jesus problem they were so concerned about. Feeling obligated to fulfill my side of the bargain, I called the desk to have them connect me to the room number the psychic lady had given me, where I'm sure I woke her. She was patient as I explained my weird dilemma, when she simply said, "all I'm getting is you need to talk to Geoff about it". She had no idea of what else could be going on, and frankly, I could tell she just wanted to grab some more shut eye before the retreat started its 2nd day.

The spirits had quieted down, so now I was afraid I would be late for the retreat if I dared try to sleep again. I was still so extremely exhausted that it felt like I was dragging a ton of steel to the shower with me. I moved so slow in getting myself ready due to my exhaustion, that I ended up arriving a little late, and had to, once again, blow off getting any food in my stomach.

To give you an idea of how spent I really was, I came very close to passing out as I was walking down the hallway to the elevator. I didn't even know a person could be that exhausted and still be moving around. I'm not sure how I even made it to the retreat room, and when I did, I just sat there throughout the morning in a daze. It's sad, because now half the retreat was over, and I'd virtually missed it because I was simply too overwhelmed by exhaustion to absorb anything. As I sat there with my head hanging low, I located Geoff in the room, but didn't want to interrupt the meeting to go talk to him.

I waited patiently all through the morning's proceedings, and as soon as they announced we were breaking for lunch, I headed to the back of the room to see if Geoff would talk to me. He suggested we go talk right then, skipping lunch, which was fine with me. I knew it wasn't fine to skip yet another meal, since I was still feeling light headed and ready to pass out anytime. I needed food or sleep or both very badly, even some coffee would have been helpful. But, it was too important a task the spirits from the night before had assigned to me, even though I had no idea why or even what they were asking me to do. I only knew I had to speak with Geoff as soon as possible in response to their desperate request for help.

It never ceases to amaze me, looking back at all this, how Spirit makes everything seem so immediately important, when Spirit takes years, even decades, to bring things to fruition. When I think back on how silly it was for me to sacrifice so much or work so hard to fulfill the tasks Spirit asked of me as quickly as possible it astounds me. Boy, would I do things differently if I had a 2nd chance at this life. I would get an extra hour of sleep and would have spoken to Geoff after lunch, just for starters.

Geoff led me to a room where we could speak privately. I told him about the message from the spirits in my room the night before, and since I wasn't even religious, I had no idea how I could help with their Jesus problem. To my disappointment, he also had no idea what the Jesus message could be about, or why I should speak to him. I could see in his eyes that he really wanted to help me, so I relaxed a bit, and remembered that other thing I was told by Lee to talk to him about.

I began to tell him about my Grand Canyon experience, when he announced he'd had a similar experience!! When I spoke of the intense Joy and Love and the way the leaves glowed, he knew exactly what I was talking about. Wow! No wonder it was Geoff I needed to speak to about this, even though I still didn't know why. I started to tell him about the all-knowingness, when he stopped me to ask if I'd experienced a depression when I came down from it. I told him I didn't, and returned to the all-knowingness part again. He stopped me again to say these words, "You are carrying a lot of wisdom within you. You should write a book."

OH MY GOD, that's it, that's why I needed to speak to Geoff, that's why I'd been getting those strange thoughts of writing a book for the past year or so. I needed to write a book about my experience and that new information I've been waiting to share ever since. Because Geoff did not seem to relate to the all-knowingness part of my experience, and even told me I was carrying around a lot of wisdom, I'm guessing that was not part of his experience. Even so, it was great to know someone else had experienced something similar, so I wasn't alone in this phenomenon.

As far as the Jesus problem is concerned, there is only one thing it can be. The spirits wanted me to fix the problem by telling "them". Clearly, the way to tell "them", I now understand, is to tell the world, YOU, by writing a book. Those spirits were trying to tell me to write a book, which is also why the "him" was Geoff, so he could put that idea clearly in my mind. After all, Spirit had been trying to tell me for quite a while now, but I was still too much an infant to realize that the strange thoughts to write a book were messages coming from Spirit.

The question remains, what does my book have to do with Jesus? As I've already told you, I spent 12 years writing that book to nowhere, which involved some very intense research into the Bible. This book you are reading now is all about Love, as you will soon see, and more on the topic of Love will be found in the books yet to come, especially my next book, <u>Echoes From Spirit</u>, since it covers the science of Love.

Love is also what Jesus tried so desperately to teach the world, but it fell on deaf ears. So, I can see how my work does relate to Jesus, and also why "it is just like it was when Jesus was here". People still do not understand the key to their salvation, Love. I will do my very best to remedy that problem with this work. Even though the world is "just like it was when Jesus was here", I'm not going to ask you to relearn what Jesus taught or try to redo what Jesus did. The spirits in my room that night were NOT asking me to. They only wanted me to fix it.

Becoming An Author

Once I got back from the spiritual retreat, all I wanted to do is get started writing my book. I knew immediately how I should write it, using the Holy Bible as backup to my truth, because of my brother, Steve. Only a couple months prior had he told me he was trying to decide which religion to follow, after studying with a couple of Mormons who had been coming to his door for a couple years. I asked him to please wait before making a final decision until I could find a book that described my truths. He agreed, but upon searching for such a book, I realized, no such book existed. Even the Kryon books never discussed what I am meant to disclose to the world.

When the realization finally dawned on me to write a book, I knew what I had to write, but I also wanted it to be a book that would help my brother. Using the Bible to prove my words was something I immediately felt I had to do, since I knew my brother wouldn't believe anything solely coming from me. I spent the next 12+ years writing and rewriting that book, researching the Bible extensively and reporting my findings in my work. When I think back on this, realizing that book never got published, I don't waste any time wondering if all those years of heavy analysis were a mistake, because of something else that happened well over 30 years ago. Without a doubt, I was meant to do that in-depth research into the Bible, since for one thing, it will come in handy in illustrating what I have to say in the books to come in this series.

As I've said, Spirit has been the driving force of my life, even long before I realized it, and I've done my best to follow that lead for 18 years now. Even so, let's face it, motivating me to actively study the Bible for 12 years took some serious doing. Since I'm not religious, and not a big reader, even picking up the Bible at all was a stretch for me. Studying it intensively, even to the point of using 5 dictionaries to research the complex verses, was only possible through divine spiritual intervention, which brings me to my next spiritual story.

Understand, this next story is nowhere near chronological order, since it made more sense to wait until I got to this point in my story to tell you about this experience. We are backing up way before Australia, to the earliest years of my relationship with my husband, in fact, only about 5 months after we were married. Hmmm, interestingly enough, that places it somewhere in April.

A Brief Encounter

This story is about a brief encounter, which in hindsight was clearly a part of the plan for my life. When I began the project to write a book, and in fact, all through my life, I've felt that the Bibles available to us today had seriously comprised the words of God. The people God initially spoke to wrote it using the Hebrew language, and the New Testament was translated from Greek. Not all the words could be translated directly, simply because there was no English word that held the same meaning. Not only that, but many chapters (or "books") were removed from today's Bible simply because the men of the time did not agree with them.

That was my justification for why the scholars from Sunday school didn't know the answers to my questions as a child. Questions like; why was I supposed to fear the one entity in all the universe who loved me beyond all else? I forgave their avoidance of my questions, assuming they didn't know the answers because the Bible had been compromised. Even so, I felt I had some inside information from my time in the all-knowingness, which gave me confidence in my new perspective that could see beyond their biblical updates. I was confident the Bible still held the truth for someone who was taught by Spirit how to read it.

With the decision made to write a book using the Bible as backup, it was time to choose a Bible. The first thought that came to mind was that it should be an "Original King James" version, since it is as original as it gets in the English language. Then I remembered that I already had a Bible, which had been given to me many years prior. It's significant that I tell you how my particular Bible came to be, so you will know why this story is part of the magic that brought me to this day.

This story is definitely a spiritual experience, making it an important part of my spiritual life and should, therefore, be included in this spiritual memoir. It explains one reason why I was so focused on researching the bible, why I would spend over 12 years trying to write a book so perfect it would pass the stringent requirements of my spiritual pact, which is another spiritual story I've yet to tell.

All of this is a very important part of what made me who I am today and what brought me to writing the book you are reading and the books I know are coming. I have learned way too much to fit in any one book, or even two books, and I'm sure I won't be done after three books either. I have much to tell, and it all started with this story long before I had any idea I would ever write any book. Spirit has been organizing my life starting from long before I was even aware of that possibility.

The Stranger

One early spring weekend afternoon, my husband and I were delighted by a surprise visit from a friend we thought we'd never see again. We'd already said our good-byes to him a couple nights before, because he was moving out of state, and should have already been gone or going on this day. If that wasn't strange enough, when our friend, named John, got out of his car, a complete stranger got out of his car with him. I thought it was a bit unusual when John didn't introduce the stranger to us or even acknowledge him in any way. So, to be polite, we introduced ourselves, and welcomed the stranger into our home along with our friend.

We went directly into our game room, where we usually entertained guests, since it was the largest room in our small 2 bedroom house. Right away, I challenged our guests to a game of pool, which became a game of partners with my husband and I on opposing teams. As soon as I got the chance, I quietly pulled my partner, John, aside and asked him who this strange guy was and how he knew him. That is when I learned he didn't know him at all. John said, "I don't know how to explain it. He just, kind of, got in the car with me as I was leaving to come... here." I could sense his own doubts as to why he'd even come to our house.

Now this was starting to get pretty weird. Not only was our friend supposed to be on his way out of state, meaning his wife is waiting for him somewhere so they can proceed as planned, but John was simply not the type of person to let a stranger get into his car, much less bring him to our house. The whole thing was way out of character for John, but to make it even more bizarre, you should have a picture of this stranger in your mind.

He was about our age, but it was hard to tell initially due to his attire. In obvious need of a bath, he wore a raggedy suit coat full of holes with a dirty shirt underneath. The truth is, he was filthy to the point of dirt showing on his face and was literally dressed in rags. He looked like he'd been homeless and on the road traveling like a hobo for quite some time.

As curious as I was about this stranger, and what John was even doing at our house, I wasn't able to ask any more questions, or tell my husband about what John had said, because, after all, it was my turn at pool. My many questions have gone unanswered to this day, because suddenly, after that first game of pool, our friend was in a big hurry to leave and we have never seen John again since that day.

His departure, in and of itself, didn't surprise us, because of course, John had to get going with his move out of state. He didn't even waste any time saying good-byes to us, since we had already been down that road, and he really was behind schedule. We understood that he needed to leave, since it was never clear why he even came, but we were very surprised that he left the stranger behind. Our heads were spinning as we wondered what in the world was going on.

There we were, standing with our jaws open as our friend bolted out the door leaving this homeless stranger in our midst. My husband and I turned to look at each other and then look at the stranger at the same time, both too stunned to say anything. The stranger simply looked right back at us and asked straight out if it would be okay if he stayed with us for a while. Even though one game of pool was far from enough to get to know someone, there was something special about this person. He was a very nice kind of guy, quiet, yet with a friendly and somewhat funny personality.

Without hesitation, or even discussion, we both agreed to allow him to stay for as long as he liked. He offered no explanation, and we never asked for one. It's true, we were always a somewhat naturally charitable couple, especially my husband, but this was way over the top, even for us. For whatever reason, we never doubted our decision to help this guy, and we have, most certainly, never regretted it.

With that settled, I put my numerous questions to the back of my mind and set out playing hostess, making him feel at home. I asked him if he was hungry, promising to whip something up for dinner soon, and told him to feel free to use the shower. Since he obviously had no clean clothes, my husband offered him some of his clothes to wear after using our shower. While my husband was heading off to get him some clothes to wear, the stranger handed me a Bible and asked me to hold it for him.

Oh brother, more questions came flooding into my mind. The most prominent among them, was where had this Bible been the entire time we were playing pool? He just pulled it out from the chest of his raggedy suit coat, a full-sized (9" x 7") leather bound Original King James Bible. How could it have been there when he was bending over to shoot the cue ball? They don't make pockets that big on any coats I've seen, and even if he had such a pocket, the coat fit him tight, so it seemed like a book that size should have been noticeable.

I put the questions behind me once again, as I took the Bible from his hand, placing it on the shelf of the coffee table in front of me. He didn't know it yet, but he was going to be sleeping on that couch in the game room, since that was all we had to offer in our small 2 bedroom house. The 2nd bedroom was only used for storage and the couch in the living room was just a love seat, not big enough to sleep on. I figured the coffee table next to where he'd be sleeping would be a good place for the Bible during his stay.

For some strange reason, looking back at this, we never asked him anything about himself throughout his stay with us, and he never offered any information. He simply said he was traveling through, but never even said how long he intended to remain, and we didn't care. Thinking back on it, my husband thought he stayed with us for a couple weeks, and he was probably right, since I remember having at least one more weekend with him when some other friends came over. Even though we never did learn anything about him, we both liked him very much and enjoyed his company. He was genuinely welcome to stay for as long as he liked.

There is another reason I think he was there for about 2 weeks. There came a day when my husband was at work and I was home on a "day off" cleaning house. This is significant, because that never happened, except for one day a year. The owners of the company I worked for were Jewish, and out of their respect for religion, they gave us an extra holiday according to whatever our religion was. The day I took off, therefore, was always Good Friday, and my husband didn't get that day off work.

I'm thinking it must have been Good Friday when the next thing happened, because I was home (and healthy, not a sick day) while my husband was at work. The interesting thing about this realization is that Good Friday is also in April. There really is something about that month and me, but I never realized it until I started putting all this information together for this book.

On this day in April, I was busy cleaning house when our new friend asked me if he could borrow a piece of paper and a pen. I gave him a stenographer's notepad and a pencil, making sure this would be sufficient for him. He said it would be fine, but then he asked me a really strange question. He wanted to know what my "real" name was. I told him my name was the name I introduced myself as, which was "Betz".

I'd been proudly using my nickname among friends ever since working at the Grand Canyon, since my brother introduced me by that name. I explained to him, that it is as much my name as the name I was born with, because I have been called it since I was in diapers. Just so you know, I reverted back to using my "real" name, Kathy, after moving to Australia, simply because it was getting old comparing my name to a vegetable, "beets". Besides, strange nicknames weren't that common among Aussies. But, my brother and my oldest friend still call me Betz to this day, which truly is my preference for those who are close to me.

Anyway, our strange friend said my nickname was good enough for him, even though I offered to tell him my "real" name. He went off and disappeared for a couple hours to do whatever he was planning to do with the paper I gave him. I hate to say it, but this disappearance brings up more questions, since there was no place in or around our house where he could have done what he ended up doing with that paper, especially with me going all over the house cleaning. I never ran into him anywhere during that time, so that has me asking more questions, which I never even thought to ask until now.

When he was done, he came into the game room, where I was still cleaning, and handed me this beautiful calligraphy with mine ("Betz") and my husband's name on it ("Larry"). In the corner, he drew a 3 dimensional book with the words, "Book of Life" on the cover. He had even gone to the trouble of burning the edges of the paper so that the paper looked old and scroll like.

I was delighted with it when I saw it, having no idea what any of it meant at the time. Remember, I'd never read the Bible in my life up to now, so even "Book of Life" meant nothing to me then. I just thought it was beautiful artwork and a very thoughtful gesture of appreciation on his part. I automatically assumed it was his way of thanking us for making him welcome in our home. With the beautiful calligraphy in hand, I smiled broadly at him with a sincere thank you, as I reached out to give him a hug of gratitude.

That's when he took me by complete surprise, because he would have none of it!! He stepped back putting his hand up flat in front of him to stop the hug, and the look on his face was very serious. His stern demeanor was letting me know that it was much more than a gesture of appreciation. He stopped me cold, and was very serious when he told me that this paper was extremely important. He said that it was crucial that I keep it forever, and that I should put it where it will be protected and in a safe place. Then he told me to put it in the Bible to keep it safe.

This was the first indication, in my mind, that he planned on leaving the Bible behind. I said, "Oh no, that's your Bible, you'll be wanting it back." There was a tone of surprise in his voice, indicating he'd never intended on taking it with him and thought I had understood that, when he said, "No, you keep it for me." I remember looking at him puzzled, because I didn't want to keep his Bible. He saw my confusion and searched for a way to help me accept his intentions to leave it by adding, "I'll be back to get it someday".

I could accept that, since even though I had no purpose for his Bible, I could see why he wouldn't want to drag it around with him during his travels, even though his true intentions were never explained. I was finally allowed to give him that hug of appreciation, but I was disappointed, because he still maintained his serious demeanor, keeping the hug brief and without emotion.

The next thing that happened was the strangest part about this entire story. As I went to put the paper away in the back of the Bible, which was still on the coffee table shelf right next to me, he turned and headed out of the game room. Not a moment later, I heard the front door of our house close. My instincts screamed at me, as I somehow knew he must be leaving.

I put the Bible down quickly and immediately followed after him, literally running through the house and out to the front yard. I desperately wanted to say a proper good-bye. That stiff hug wasn't enough for a good-bye, especially since I didn't know it was to be the last time I would see him. But he was already gone from sight. Right out of the blue, he disappeared. I remember he was still wearing my husband's clothes when I last saw him.

To this day, I have no idea how or where he went. Remember, he had no car, and we lived quite a long way out of town in the middle of a block of houses, all with fences. I wasn't that far behind him as I ran straight through the house, which was only 2 small rooms with no obstacles or corners slowing me down. I threw the front door open and ran directly out into the street to look for him.

But when I got there, I found no trace of him or of anyone else, for that matter. There wasn't a single car, person or even animal in sight in either direction. No sounds either, no barking dogs. He was completely gone with no trace. He didn't have time to walk out of sight, or run out of sight, or even drive away in a cab, without me spotting him leaving. He simply disappeared from our lives in that instant without so much as a good-bye.

All we have to remember him by is the Bible he wanted me to "hold for him", and the Calligraphy with the "Book of Life" drawn in the corner. Which, by the way, he signed, even though I can't read his name. It doesn't look anything like the name he gave us, which is why I don't refer to him by that name, and it was only a first name we knew him by anyway. Maybe a professional handwriting analyst can tell me his name someday.

I've included a high quality image of his artwork below for you to ponder over yourself. I am hoping someone will be able to help me solve the mystery of what makes this paper so important. There are some markings, or letters, or what could even be phrases, on the binding of the "Book Of Life" he drew in the corner. If you know someone proficient in languages or a handwriting specialist who can read his signature, perhaps you can help me solve the mystery.

If your expertise goes along these lines and you think you can help decipher this mysterious calligraphy, I'd love to hear from you. If you need a better look at it in the original colors, rather than the gray scale version I've had to include here, you will find a copy of it on my website at www.eagle-awareness.com. I am also including a link to it in the references section of this book. Of course, there are copyright laws protecting it, so please do not copy it. I am actually taking that risk myself, because I would welcome him to come forward, but I'm sure he would be angry to see it anywhere outside of my work.

Isn't it interesting, that over the years the lines of the page from the stenographer's notebook have almost completely disappeared? I remember thinking how unusual I thought this particular paper was when I bought it, but it was the only style they had at the time. The paper was a light green and the lines were white, plus there was no line down the middle as is normally the case with this kind of notebook. I've never seen this style again even though I've always used this type of notebook for my travel logs and more. Once again, Spirit put what I needed in my hands, this time a style of paper that would not interfere with the artwork meant to be drawn on it.

Notice that next to his signature he wrote some numbers denoting the year, "79". That was 36 years ago, and since then we have moved several times, literally all over the world, but the Bible always came with us. Even though Bibles weren't my thing, I still packed it and repacked it, because, you see, I was keeping it for him. Without a doubt, if he wouldn't have told me he would be back for it someday, I'm sure I would have thrown it out or given it away at some point over these long years, because the thought to do so came to mind often. When it did, however, I would remember that it wasn't my Bible to give away.

What would I say to him if I ever did see him again? How could I tell him that I threw away the Bible he put into my care? I had way too much respect for that man to do that, but even as I say that, I don't know why I felt that way about him. Since then, however, my respect for him has grown much stronger for reasons you will understand soon.

Back To The Present

Now let's return to the present, or at least, to when I first set out to write a book expecting the Bible to be backup evidence of my truth. With that story nothing more than a distant memory of a "stranger" we once knew briefly, I finally opened the Bible I had been carrying around with us all over the world. The first thing I discovered in the Bible was that calligraphy he had done with our names on it.

That was actually the first time I noticed the foreign markings he had drawn on the binder of that "Book of Life" in the corner. I tried looking them up on the internet with no luck. I still, to this day, don't know what they mean, but I have a strong feeling they are very important, and could even be why he told me to keep that paper always safe. After all, how many disappearing angels leave physical evidence of their visit behind?

When I had a good look at this stranger's Bible, I discovered that it is literally full of notations clarifying the original Greek and Hebrew words, even the occasional Arabic word, along with their meanings. There are numerous verses underlined in red, and with word corrections, and even new verse references, which helped me tremendously in studying the Bible.

Now that I have read a good portion of that Bible, I realize, that all those subtle little changes he has made or enhanced here and there, are literally telling me what was in the original text, correcting any errors the transcribers may have made! It didn't hit me right away, when I saw the strange looking words on the binder of the book he drew, but seeing all the Hebrew, Greek and sometimes Arabic words he has written in this Bible, made me realize how truly profound that individual was.

Think about it. That man was literally dressed in rags, and yet he was a serious scholar of the Holy Bible, obviously and to say the very least. So much a scholar, in fact, that he fluently knew Greek, Hebrew and Arabic even in their ancient forms! It's as if the calligraphy was provided as proof that it was him who did the work inside the Bible, since it has those strange words on the binding of the drawn book. Why that would matter can only be known once we can read his name, which I have a strong feeling may also be very telling.

With disappearing strangers and the like, I guess you could say God truly does work in strange ways. Before we put too much into that thought pattern, however, I have a question for you, to get you thinking again and to help you keep your assumptions at bay. My question is; who are you assuming this stranger was? Do you think he was an angel? Perhaps, and that was my first assumption as well, but after all these years I've realized there is more than that one possibility.

What if the reason I didn't see him leave is because I didn't look up? Could it be within the realm of possibility that his transportation was a space ship? I know it sounds crazy, but I risk sounding crazy for a reason. Because, one thing I know for sure is assumptions are not healthy. All any of us can do to be sure is wait until the day comes when he returns to retrieve his Bible. I have a whole lot of questions begging for answers from that man as I continue to wait for that day to come.

The Book To Nowhere

It may seem strange, that Spirit would deliver me a Bible, and then send me on what now appears to have been a wild goose chase. To have studied the Bible with such intensity for so long only to have all that work never get published seems like such a waste. It was a very interesting and enlightening journey, so it was well worth it, but I now understand, it won't go to waste. What brought me to that conclusion is actually a story that is still unfolding, so I don't know where to begin with this one.

I initially thought it was my job to bring the truths I was discovering in the Bible to the surface through my one book. Even though the Bible does include some of the truths I was shown in the all-knowingness, it doesn't state it clearly, and I was shown more than what the Bible even discloses. But, the Bible is full of its own truths, things that not only enhance or even clarify what I already knew, but also things I'd never thought of before, because I'd never dealt with it before. Things specifically related to religion or the religious way of looking at things.

Just to be clear for those who are dying to know, when I was in the all-knowingness, religion was not even close by. There was no God up there with me to meet, and no Spirit of Jesus, no Holy Ghost, no heaven or hell, none of it. I was being shown the SCIENCE of our reality in the all-knowingness, and then I was taken on a religious journey through studying the Bible. Because I was shown the science first, and in a way that left me with absolutely no doubts as to the accuracy of what I know, I was able to see the truths of the Bible with a new perspective. This made it possible, even necessary, to combine science with religion so I could see the FULL TRUTH of mankind and the realities of our existence.

I learned recently that it was way back in the late 1800's, when Pope Leo the 13th firmly asserted the doctrine that science and religion coexist. I have to wonder what happened to such wisdom. People want to so easily throw science away in favor of "faith", as if clarifying their understanding of what they have faith in is sac-religious or something. And the men of science treat religion as some sort of fairy tale only ignorant people believe in. Well, my brother, the one I wanted to help, is very intelligent and very religious. I have to say I couldn't help him, at least not yet, because it has taken me this long to understand what Spirit was trying to train me to do.

You are probably wondering what took me so long to figure out the obvious. It has been 14 years ago now, that I first sat down to write the book to nowhere. When I did, I expected my truth to be there waiting for me, and it was. But without any way of proving that to people, I became frustrated and confused over what Spirit was asking me to do. I started diving in deeper, always searching for the proof I needed to convince people that the way I was perceiving the Bible was the truth.

I finally came to realize, that the Bible really isn't the best resource to use for backup proof of the new information I am meant to share with the world. The interesting thing about this whole journey I'm on, is while I was busy studying the Bible and thinking I was doing the work I was supposed to do for Spirit, the real backup proof I need to help me unveil the information I am meant to share has materialized on its own while I wasn't looking. It's called SCIENCE.

Amazing as it may seem, science is finally beginning to discover what I was shown over 40 years ago. I only need their recent scientific experiments to backup what I have to tell the world. Finally, science and religion can coexist, because the one no longer has to compromise the other. It was Albert Einstein who said, "Science without religion is lame, religion without science is blind". It is my job to show you how the two coincide, so we no longer have to be either lame or blind. But first let me tell you how my journey brought me to this conclusion.

Spiritual Pact

I'm sure, by now, you have to be wondering what took me so long. What made me spend 12 years studying a Bible and writing a book, just to have it never be seen by the public? What was it going to take for me to finally decide it was time to publish the book I'd spent over a decade researching and writing? What on earth would keep someone working so hard and for so long on something, and then be willing to just let it die? It's time I tell you that story, another profound spiritual experience.

Throughout this entire process, there has been nothing as important to me as getting it right. As I said, when I would be shown something, or receive a message, I always needed proof. Because I was so skeptical, requiring proof at every turn, I was a very difficult servant for Spirit to work with, but I recommend everyone maintain a similar healthy skepticism. It's much healthier for us to doubt with a mind open to proof, then to follow anything with blind faith, especially the unprovable. On that note, there is still this major and very important spiritual experience I have to tell you about. The story about a pact I had with Spirit and how that came to be.

When I first started that book to nowhere, within the first few weeks, some of the verses in the Bible I thought I was being asked to write about shocked me and made me very upset. I realized the controversial bomb shell I was being asked to write. I pushed myself away from the keyboard, ran out to the living room, and started pacing the floor. I started talking to Spirit out loud (at home alone). I told him this was crazy, the world was not ready for this, they will want me dead. At the time I started that book the world wasn't ready for what I was being shown to write. Not even close, even though the world has changed dramatically since then whether you realize it or not.

I didn't get any answers to my dilemma that day, nor did I expect them, either from Spirit or from within myself. I stewed for the rest of the day, not returning to the keyboard, as I thought about what I was being asked to do. What I was truly facing was condemnation from the people I love and from the entire world, even to the point of having to accept the very real risk to my survival, all for the sake of the truth. It was quite a daunting thing to realize, that I was setting myself up for the worst possible ridicule and could be facing my own death as well. After all, they were killing doctors in abortion clinics at the time. The last thing the hard core religious leaders out there wanted was the truth exposing their confusion to the world.

After thinking about it overnight, I decided I would be willing to die for the truth. After all, getting the truth out to the world was what I had agreed to do when I had that experience in the Grand Canyon, that very important responsibility I worked hard at returning to the physical realm to fulfill. When you are actually facing the reality of giving up your life for the truth square on, it is something you don't dare take too lightly. But, I knew the truth is that important, and my life held no importance in comparison to getting the truth out there.

What worried me, however, and what made this so difficult, was having the confidence in my ability to get it all put down on paper correctly. I knew what I was shown in my Grand Canyon experience was the absolute truth, but the Bible goes into many more things that I wasn't shown, and I still wasn't trusting my own ability to get beyond those

Vision Of Truth

Sunday school "spots" (as the Bible puts it) enough to see beyond them to the complete truth.

Once I knew for sure, that I was ready to risk my life for this work, I went back into the living room to have another conversation with Spirit (seemed like the place to be, I guess). There was one very important factor in all this. If I was going to risk my life for the truth, then I needed to be ABSOLUTELY POSITIVE that it was a completely accurate Truth, and written when and how Spirit wanted me to write it, that I was risking my life for. Since I still doubted myself, this was a difficult part of the equation. So, I put a demand forward to Spirit, like any such difficult servant would do. I put a condition on my publishing that book I was about to write.

I obviously knew, from the numerous spiritual experiences I'd already had, that Spirit was capable of giving me a substantial vision. So, I told Spirit in the living room that day that I would only publish the book if I were given absolute proof, upon its completion, that it was written exactly how and when it should be written. I wanted a vision beyond any vision or experience I'd had to date, even specifying a preference for one that would incorporate all of the senses.

I didn't just want a vision of sight, as in the Medicine cards reader, or of sound, as in my sweet Angel's voice. I wanted a vision of both sight and sound, and even smell, or taste, or whatever other sense Spirit could send me. I wanted a vision so profound that there would be NO DOUBT what-so-ever remaining in my mind, that the book I had written was the absolute Truth of God, and written exactly how and when Spirit wanted it to be published for the eyes of the world to see. With this condition clearly stated, and without waiting for or expecting a response, I went back to the keyboard to continue my work on the book.

It wasn't long, maybe an hour or so later, before I was feeling apologetic for being so demanding to Spirit. After all, I had just given an ultimatum to God! Who do I think I am? I'd promised I would deliver this information to the world, so I just had to stand up and do it without placing conditions on it. So, I got up from the keyboard again, and went back to the living room, as if that were the only place where I could talk to Spirit that day.

I was just entering the room again, only starting to say the words out loud, "I'm sorr.....", when I was stopped in my tracks by a slap on my face!! That's right; I FELT a slap on my face!! Wow!! That's one sense I hadn't experienced spiritually prior to this, the sense of touch. I literally felt a slap on my face (soft and gentle touch), which even turned my head 90 degrees. With my head still turned from the slap, I immediately heard these stern words loud and clear, "HOW DARE YOU DOUBT ME, YOU WILL RECEIVE AS YOU ASKED!!"

Whoa!! Okaaayyy fine. Message heard loud and clear. A pact with Spirit was now ground in stone as far as I was concerned. I will write that book for as long as it takes until I receive the vision I had asked for, and I will never doubt Spirit again!

As it turned out, this pact with Spirit became more of a curse than a privilege. It meant I could type away at my book until my fingers bled and I still couldn't publish anything until I received that vision, a vision that never came. I now understand that it was one way in which Spirit forced my mouth shut. What I knew could not be released to the world until the science to back it up existed. Yet, even as I say that, the scientists are struggling with their latest discoveries.

The scientists are realizing, according to the internet, that if their new discoveries are true, then they must have something else wrong somewhere. They are literally even starting to put their widely accepted laws of physics back on the drawing board, and are beginning to question Einstein's theory of General Relativity. I'm here to tell them, they don't have to do all that. They do have something wrong, but it's not that difficult. I'm not only here to clarify religion to the general population, but I'm meant to clarify the new science to the scientists. This is all I have to say on this topic for now, since it is too much to include in this book. You will have to read the rest of the books in my series to see the whole picture I am meant to reveal.

I Am Kryon

The next spiritual story I'm going to tell you about happened shortly after the pact I described above was established. It starts out with me just going around the house here and there doing some house work. Suddenly, out of the blue, I heard these words clearly, "I am Kryon". It took me by such a surprise, that the skeptic in me took the forefront, so I responded out loud with the words, "Oh yeah, right" in as sarcastic a voice as I could muster. Then I heard the words again, "I am Kryon".

For whatever reason, I was in no mood for this, and was getting aggravated by this intrusion. So, I tried to chase it away with the words, "I don't believe you. If you want me to believe it, you're gonna have to prove it to me, and I mean within 24 hours." There I go again, being the demanding servant.

I don't know what or who I thought it was if it wasn't Kryon, but truthfully, I just didn't feel worthy of a visit from Kryon. I didn't know why he would come to me. I hadn't asked him to come, or anybody else, for that matter. I couldn't justify this in my mind, so the skeptic in me needed proof before I would be open to listening to anything else this visitor had to say. With that demand for proof, the voice went quiet, so I figured I'd managed to chase the intrusion away. I just shook it off as a weird fluke, and went on with my day, deciding to forget about the whole thing.

In less than an hour, I received a phone call. It was from a very good customer who had bought a lot from me in the past. He was in desperate need of some supplies, but was located at a Powwow he was a vendor at. He was asking me to please send him what he needed by express post to the Powwow. Normally, I would never do this for a few reasons.

First, he was a customer who always paid by check, and didn't even have a credit card, so he was asking me to send him the goods without getting paid first, which I NEVER did. Plus, the order was fairly large, and would therefore be heavy, meaning I would have to pay a lot of money out of pocket for the express post shipping, another thing I just would NEVER do. He promised he'd pay me as soon as he got home, but it was still something I definitely did not want to do. Among those other reasons, I just didn't want to do all this rushing around for one order for one customer when my employee wasn't there to help me. Remember, I'm handicapped, so this was a huge effort for me. I REALLY did not want to do this.

That is what was really weird about this experience. It felt like I was not in control of my actions. I heard myself tell this customer I would do it, but couldn't believe I'd done that. Now I had to fill this order and rush around to pack it and take it to the post office, spend my own out of pocket money for express post, which was over $40 in shipping expense, just because I'd told him I would. All the way through the process of doing this task, I wanted to stop and not go through with it. I tried to find an excuse I could give him later, since this was way before cell phones were in everybody's pocket. No part of me wanted to do this, and yet I did it, almost like it was an out of body experience watching myself do things entirely against my will.

With the task done, I was on my way home from the post office, when I pulled up to a stop light. That is when I was reminded of the demand I'd put on that voice earlier, that he'd better prove to me that he was Kryon within 24 hours if he wanted me to believe it. There ahead of me, on the back bumper of the car in front of me at the stop light, was my sign, my proof.

This may sound like some pretty lame proof to some people, but understand, it was not just what I was seeing, but what I was being reminded of at exactly the same moment. I wasn't reminding myself, I was being reminded by Spirit. There in front of me, on the back bumper of that car, was a big gold crown on a deep purple background.

I knew immediately what that gold crown represented. It WAS Kryon. Remember, that is how Cyndy described what she was seeing at the Cyndy party when Kryon came to her. All of a sudden, I understood why I had to go through all this hassle of rushing to put this order together for this customer. It was so that Kryon could deliver the proof to me within the 24 hours I'd demanded. If I would have stayed home, as I usually do, there would have been no way to prove it to me.

Becoming An Author

Kryon did come to me and introduced himself to me that day, and to prove it to me, as I had insisted he do, he influenced my decision making process to the point that I went completely against my own normal inclinations to fulfill that customer's rush order. That customer never paid me for that order, by the way, and never ordered from me again. I heard shortly afterwards that he'd become very ill and died. I even wondered if he was already sick at the time I received that order, if he was even at that Powwow, since I could never reach him again.

I know this sounds a bit scary, to think a Spirit could come and basically take you over. I already told you, I think he does that with Lee on occasion, whether Lee is aware of it or not. Remember though, Kryon isn't just any Spirit. He is an Archangel, and the same Spirit who spoke to Moses, making it more of an honor than an inconvenience to be visited by him. Remember also, I'd turned my life over to Spirit, so I volunteered for this.

And yet, I was being unreceptive when Kryon came to me and introduced himself, which I now regret highly. I also am the one who put out the demand to Spirit, namely Kryon in this case, to prove his identity to me within 24 hours. Therefore, I did choose this, and even demanded it, so Spirit was only doing as I had asked.

My reaction also, when I realized what had just happened, was one of delight. I was happy to know why I'd just gone through all the hassle of filling that order, and not the least bit put out by the realization that Spirit had been running the entire show. Understand; when I turned my life over to Spirit, I meant it with every fiber of my being, and have never regretted it or faltered from that stance. So, to experience such a direct contact with Spirit, even to this degree, was wonderful to me, and not scary in the least.

The sad thing is, with my skepticism put at rest, knowing absolutely, it was Kryon who had come to me that day, I've never had Kryon come and introduce himself again since. This makes me wonder, why did he come? What was his message for me? Did he have a message? I was worried that my skepticism had closed my mind, so the only thing I was able to hear was the introduction, when he said "I am Kryon". I wondered if I'd had an open mind what else he would have said.

All these years later, as I gather together the jigsaw pieces of my life for this book, I'm realizing now for the first time, that Kryon wouldn't leave me hanging without completely expressing his message. This is why I think this relates to the story I just told you, why I'm putting it in the same section, because the energy was the same. Something with a forceful energy slapped me that day in my living room, a force so strong it even turned my head, and spoke to me in what sounded like the same voice as the one I heard on this day. I believe he did give me his entire message that day. The message was, "I am Kryon". He was letting me know what entity I'd actually made that pact with. I'd made a pact with the same Spirit who had spoken to Moses on the mountain, the one Moses called GOD.

Now, we could argue until the cows come home whether Kryon is God or not. It was Moses assuming the voice he spoke to was God, not the Spirit declaring it. Kryon will tell you who God is, and it is NOT him. So, understand that first and foremost. Kryon insists it is within human beings where God is found, which is something I leave you to agree with or not, at least for now. Kryon tells us he is simply part of the family of Michael the Archangel, whom has never lived as a human being. He defines an Archangel as a family of angels, not one of greater importance as we assume.

Becoming An Author

So, I guess we could say; I made that pact with Michael the Archangel, a very powerful energy indeed. Even though Kryon is not God, he is a very powerful angel whom I respect highly. I just want you to understand, I would never break that pact I made with him to my dying day, not out of fear in any sense of the word, but out of respect.

If I spend the rest of my days, writing and rewriting a book that never goes to a publisher, waiting in suffering for a vision that never comes, then so be it. I would rather go through that, as I have been for 14 years of waiting up to now, than break a pact resulting in publishing a book the world wasn't ready to see. Even with that said, however, I know I am meant to write the series of books I am writing. I won't be waiting for a vision to publish them either, at least not most of them.

Understand, these books do not break that pact. The pact I made was to not publish the book I was writing, where the Bible was showing me truths the world wasn't ready to hear. The world is still not entirely ready for that depth of disclosure. I will still keep that information to myself until I do receive my promised vision releasing me from the pact. Only Spirit knows when the world will be ready. In the meantime, I now know I have to share what I was shown in the Grand Canyon experience, which will lead up to the controversial information I was shown in the Bible. It will prepare the world for the full disclosure, which I will only release once that vision comes.

Believe me, if you continue to follow me in this journey, you will know when that vision comes, since it will likely be astounding enough to fill a book all on its own. It will also be when my work takes a major turn in another direction. Just understand, that in the meantime, I will be referring to the Bible verses on occasion, when it can clearly support a point I am trying to make without having to get too deeply into my intense research. This should help you see how science and religion can coexist and even support each other.

My pact doesn't block me from referring to the basic concepts of religion. It only blocks me from exposing what my in-depth research revealed to me. It took me a long time to realize that, however, which is why it has taken me so long to finally begin releasing what I was shown to the world. What I have to teach in the books to follow should not conflict with any doctrine out there. So, if at any point you get that impression, please let it go, because that is simply not where I am coming from.

This work is outside of that pact, not bound by the conditions I myself laid out. How I came to realize I was free to publish this information is another story I'm about to tell. In truth, visible only in hindsight, I can see now that I was being kept silent for a reason, because humanity wasn't ready for anything I had to say, until now.

Dealing With Dilemmas

With the complete understanding, by now, that it was possible to connect with Spirit in a very real way, I set out trying to establish a connection as a means of finding answers to the many questions my research was uncovering. As the writing of that book to nowhere progressed, my connection with Spirit grew stronger. In fact, writing the book, especially in the early days, was a spiritual experience in and of itself making it completely impossible to include every spiritual thing that has happened to me in this memoir.

Realize, what I am talking about now is a connection with my own higher self, which some would consider their own soul. What we need to remember, first and foremost, is the best way to define a human being is as an eternal spiritual soul and consciousness on a brief physical journey. If you can TRY to accept as completely as I know, that WE ARE ONE, then you should be able to understand, when I say, that to speak to your own higher self IS to speak to Spirit, or God. THEY are One.

My Situation

That spiritual experience putting a pact in place with Michael the Archangel, even involving a new sense, the sense of touch, and being combined with the sense of hearing through my ears, as with my sweet angel years ago, was enough to carry me in faith all these years. I was sure I was meant to write the book and do the research. That, to me, was an absolute pact I now had with Spirit. I would do as I was directed, write a book using the Bible as proof of my words, and wait until I received my promised vision before considering the book ready for publishing.

The problem is; I took my pact with Spirit so serious, that I went far beyond what the pact had specified. Since that day, I've thought without a doubt, that NO book would ever be published by me until after I have had that vision I asked for and was promised I "WILL RECEIVE". I was so bound by that pact with Spirit, that it stopped me from moving forward with any spiritual pursuits. I thought the publishing of that book would be where my spiritual purpose and life would begin. Plus, I was constantly assuming my spiritual approval would be right around the corner, just after my next edit or additional research.

Like I said, assumptions are a huge problem, and I was assuming way too much. I was so sure of my assumptions, having ground them in stone after 12 years of waiting for them to be fulfilled, that I was ready to literally go to my grave without ever having a spiritual life of any kind if that vision never came. In fact, that is exactly where I was headed, due to my handicap. It's finally time I tell you about my physical journey including my handicap and more. There are some relevant spiritual messages that relate to my condition, so Spirit has a part in this chapter of my story as well.

My Handicap

It is because of my handicap that my assumptions were held so strongly in place. You see, I thought I would have to overcome my condition long before the book I was writing could be published. It had to be, because I was telling people how to overcome their problems, and yet I was burdened by a huge problem myself, and one people automatically assume is my own fault.

How could anyone believe what I had to say, someone with such an obvious condition people instantly judge to be a personality flaw rather than a handicap. I now realize that people will have to SEE me, which was something Spirit told me at the start of writing my book, even though I didn't hear it until years later. I'll get to that story in chronological order, but first it's time I tell you what that means, to warn you of what you might see when that day comes.

My handicap is extreme morbid obesity, currently weighing about 450 lbs. Before you judge, please hear me out first. I never had a weight problem in my youth, even though I always had a bad body image due to ridicule from my brother, Steve, always telling me I was fat. In truth, I wasn't fat, not even close, but I did have what my mother called "big bones". That assessment only made matters worse, since I figured my mother was only finding a gentle way of agreeing with my brother. My body image was horrible, but I was wrong. Looking at pictures from long ago, I now know that I was very attractive, standing 5'9" with long legs and hips substantial enough to be considered graciously endowed with curves, but never fat, not even overweight.

When I was about 16 years old, our family doctor told me I had a thyroid condition. I learned later that both my mother and her mother also had that same condition and had been taking thyroid medication all their lives. Our doctor, however, felt I was too young to be starting me on a life sentence of taking drugs, so he just told me to "keep an eye on it because it WILL get worse". Problem is, our doctor was a man of few words, so nobody ever told me what a thyroid condition even was. How was I supposed to keep an eye on it?

I always did have to struggle extra hard to shed pounds when I felt the need, but I didn't know why it was harder for me than most people. It turned from difficult to impossible by the time we had a house fire when I was in my 30's. The insurance company put us up in a motel for 3 months while our house was going through a major overhaul, and they paid for every meal we had at restaurants the entire time. I enjoyed every minute of it, all the luscious meals and the delectable desserts they often included. I figured I would just lose the weight later, but that was a hurdle I never could achieve. Still oblivious to what it means to have a thyroid condition, I not only couldn't lose the weight, but dieting even caused me to gain more weight. My body had taken a serious turn for the worst.

Back To My Guru

By the time we moved to Australia about 5-6 years later, I was exceeding 250 lbs., which is actually less than 100 lbs. over my ideal weight, since remember, I am very tall and big boned. By the time my Guru came to visit me in my shop 3 years after our move, I was probably exceeding 300 pounds. I was never sure of my weight though, since scales don't go that high, but I was definitely having a problem and it was getting worse. Understand, please, it wasn't because I've ever had an over-eating disorder.

Dealing With Dilemmas

Even though food has never been a crutch or over eating a problem, I do have what most would consider an eating fault. I have a strong distaste for vegetables and I've never been too excited about fruit either. This made finding food I could eat to lose weight very difficult. My solution was to just not eat, or just barely eat enough to stay alive. In other words, I'm not an over eater, never have been. But I think my approach to dieting actually made my thyroid condition worse. One thing is sure, my starvation approach caused my body to hold on tight to my fat reserves, a reality not yet understood by science at the time.

When my Guru came into my shop that day, I had some questions for him regarding my weight problem. The actual reading was finished, when I asked him, "will I ever be able to lose this excess weight I'm carrying around?" At the time, I could still get around pretty good since I was so much younger then. That was about 19 years ago now, so I was only about 42 years old.

As soon as I asked him this question, he looked at me with a very serious look on his face, as he told me it will get worse before it gets better. But then, he said, "Someone will come help you lose the weight you need to lose to do what you need to do." He let me know I wouldn't lose it all, by telling me, "You'll never be a Barbie doll." He then repeated, "It will get worse before it gets better, a lot worse. But, finally someone will come to you, and he will help you lose the weight you need to lose to do what you need to do." I was okay with that, since I never have been a vain person, so I didn't care about what others thought, and my husband loved me regardless.

All I wanted was to be able to do the things I wanted to do, like ride horses or go camping in comfort, and it sounded to me like he was telling me that would happen.

But, that isn't what he was telling me. He was talking about losing enough weight to do what I would "need to do", NOT what I wanted to do. My assumptions were already hard at work. He knew I was assuming things, because he didn't seem so delighted for me. I figured he was concerned about it getting worse first, never guessing how bad it could get.

During the reading itself, prior to my asking any questions, he told me I would have a hard time walking due to a problem with my joints. My assumptions, when he told me that, were that he was talking about when I reach old age. I'm telling you, assumptions are a very serious problem, since they take their place in your thoughts without you having any awareness of them, and they cause you to do things you wouldn't otherwise do. Because I was assuming it was old age he was talking about, I never bothered to ask him when it would happen, or even how.

Sure enough, shortly after returning to America, I injured my knee and was forced to start walking with a cane. That knee injury, which was aggravated by a couple falls with all my weight landing, first on one knee and then on the other, lessened my mobility substantially. As the years have gone on, my ability to get around decreased more and more, until I am now very dependent on an electric power chair. My immobility added to the weight problem, which added to the joint problem, which added to the weight problem, and around and around it accelerated for all these years since.

These days I have trouble with all my joints to some degree, and due to pain from severe inflammation my mobility is to the point that I am completely home bound. My Guru has been 100% accurate in his reading to date, but so far, it's all been bad. I'm still waiting for the good news he promised, for that help to lose weight and the spiritual success I was told I would achieve.

From when we first came back to America I started trying to find that person who was supposed to come help me lose the weight. I was justifying my efforts by remembering my Guru didn't specify that I wouldn't recruit the help, even though my instincts told me that wasn't how it will happen. The first thing I did is try to contact Richard Simmons, the famous diet and exercise expert, but all that brought me was a bunch of his company products with no direct help from him.

I tried everything I could think of over the years, including hiring a personal trainer to come to my house 3 times a week, which was very expensive and brought zero results. I also approached a scientist who was familiar with Kryon, thinking maybe it was a spiritual thing he could help me with. He did his best, but again, no help. All these efforts were lacking one very important component I always knew was missing, which caused me concern and likely even undermined my efforts.

The missing component was that they were always attempts to lose the weight by normal means. Everyone expected me to lose the weight by diet and/or exercise, but I knew in my heart, that was not how I am meant to achieve my weight loss. I know, this sounds crazy, which is why I could never tell anyone what I knew in my heart. But I had good reason to feel this way, which brings me to my next spiritual story.

By A Miracle

Going back again to within the first months of writing the book to nowhere, I was really starting to wonder why I was having so much trouble losing weight, still completely unaware of what a thyroid condition is. My weight problem was getting worse already, as my Guru said it would, since I'd gained another 50 pounds or so by then. Losing patience for the promised someone to come help me lose the weight, I turned to Spirit for some answers.

By this time, I was getting pretty good at communicating with Spirit, since I was trying to perfect that connection as a means of gaining guidance in writing the book. It was to the point that all I had to do is quiet my mind, and the answers would come fairly quickly. I started asking Spirit when and how I was going to lose weight. I did this repeatedly over several weeks, but didn't get any answers at first.

Finally, I got an answer, but didn't understand it, so I continued to ask the same question again and again. Repeatedly, three times in a row, I got the same exact message, and then the answers stopped. Like I said earlier, things often come to me in 3's. I don't know what it is, but the number 3 and the month of April seem to be keys for me.

The exact wording I got in my message from Spirit in answer to my question of when and how I was going to lose my weight was this, "it will be as if by a miracle and many people will see it". My question was covering both how I would lose the weight, and when. The how answer came first with "it will be as if by a miracle", and the 2nd part of the same message told me it would be when "many people will see it". Not much of an answer is it? You can probably see why I still continued to ask the question.

After at least a decade of trying to lose the weight on my own and trying to force that help I was told would come, I had to finally surrender to the realization that my weight problem must also have a divine purpose. I had to accept, that the help will come when it is time and nothing

I can do will force that process. These conditions, set by that message from Spirit, are what made the efforts I was making on my own seem pointless. Even the spiritual scientist was trying to help me by normal means of diet and exercise. How is that "as if by a miracle"? And it also never fit that "many people will see it" part of the message. I knew those conditions Spirit described could not be forced. I had no choice but to surrender to my destiny.

Fake Name

As my efforts to finish the book to nowhere continued, and years passed, while the help to lose the weight never came, something finally dawned on me. Having already realized that my weight condition was part of my destiny, I thought it was likely that the message telling me that "many people will see it" meant that I wouldn't lose the weight until after the book was published, since that would likely be a reason people would see me.

I was living a very low key existence, with just me and my husband. Our only visitor was the maid who came a couple hours a week. This made the likelihood of "many people" seeing me extremely low. The only thing that made sense to me, was that publishing the book would bring the attention of "many people". Once I came to that conclusion, it wasn't long before another realization hit me. I finally put two and two together regarding another message I'd received from Spirit years earlier.

It was shortly after my pact was established, when I was joking with a friend about how much the holier-than-thou people of this Bible belt we live in were going to want me dead once this controversial bomb shell I was writing did get published. This was still very early on in the process and I was still under the assumption I was writing it as it should be, so it would be published right away. After all, why would I be writing a book that never gets published? It never even occurred to me, that Spirit would make me wait so long, or even at all.

Since I didn't really want to die, and I knew this really was a possibility, an alternative option came to mind. When I threw it by my friend during a phone conversation, we thought the solution would be to publish it under a fictitious "pen" name. After all, Mark Twain wasn't his name, and authors do that all the time, so why couldn't I? That way, the Bible beaters couldn't find me to kill or even harass me, leaving me safely hidden away while still achieving my goal of getting the truth out there. It sounded like a good plan, and my friend agreed, so I was trying to come up with a good fake name to use, when I received a message from Spirit.

This message came out of the blue like that message from Kryon introducing himself did, so it could have been a message from Kryon, but that was never clarified for me. It was definitely much stronger and clearer than when I would purposely try to converse with my own higher self. In looking back at this, I do believe it was Kryon. It's making me realize that Kryon was with me quite a bit during those early days of writing.

The message started out with a strong sensation that I couldn't use a fake name. Then I heard actual words, "they have to see you to believe it". Wow, okay, so that plan to use a "pen" name won't work. I had to accept that I was just going to have to face whatever publishing that work would bring and trust that Spirit would take care of me. It was obviously important that I use my real name, but my immediate reaction was to assume the reason was so that people could ask me questions and the like. I assumed Spirit was letting me know, that people wouldn't believe the truth I was writing if the person who wrote the book couldn't be found. Of course, it made sense, as our assumptions usually do.

Like I said, I was sure I would have to overcome my weight problem long before the book I was writing could be published, expecting that promised help to show up any day now. That's why I didn't really hear the message, that people would have to "see me" before they would "believe it". I realize now, Spirit doesn't mix words. If people would have needed to ask me questions before they would "believe it", then that is what the message would have been. That's not what Spirit told me, but it was several years before I put that together placing the assumptions of it's meaning behind me forever.

Spirit told me that day, many years before I could actually hear it, that for whatever reason, people have to see me as I am. Or maybe they have to see me lose the weight to believe my words. Either way, I came to realize that the help to lose the weight wasn't going to come until after the book is published. At this point, there could still be years of waiting ahead of me, because I have a lot of writing to do, and I don't know when I will have written enough for people to finally notice my work. Remember also, I established the condition myself in that pact, that the vision should come AFTER I completed the book.

Miracles Happen

When Spirit said my weight loss will be "as if" by a miracle, he was saying it would appear to be a miracle to someone, but in true reality it won't be a miracle. The question is, in whose reality? Each person's reality is limited by what they imagine their world is, but the true reality of this universe includes much more than what people can imagine. People who can't explain how they survived a car accident understand that there is more out there controlling outcomes in our lives than what we can see. We don't have to understand it or believe it for it to be true.

The dictionary defines a miracle as *"an event that appears to be neither a part nor a result of any known natural law or agency and is therefore often attributed to a supernatural source."* The key words in this definition are *"any known natural law"*. What about the unknown natural laws? Just because we don't understand the science behind an event, we decide it must be a miracle. What if there is a science behind miracles? Isn't something that is considered as *"supernatural"* just something that we haven't defined the *"natural law"* of science surrounding it yet?

Just because we don't know the science behind something doesn't make it impossible. Back in those days when the accepted science was that the earth was flat, was it impossible for Columbus to sail into the horizon without falling off the planet? Of course not. So then, was it a miracle that he ended up sailing all the way to a new found continent? No, he was just someone who pushed the boundaries of the known laws of science, which were assumptions that the earth was flat, when it was not.

What if there is a science behind luck and there is no such thing as coincidence? What if the point of miracles is to help humanity open their mind to the sciences still misunderstood or yet undiscovered? In truth, there is no such thing as a miracle, because a miracle is simply the *"supernatural"* presenting itself, which is only an undiscovered or misunderstood *"natural law"*.

The next couple stories are two very different forms of miracles. The first one would likely be considered a coincidence by the cynics, but the second will convince those same cynics that I must be delusional. This book is not one a cynic would want to read anyway, so it doesn't matter. A sceptic is someone maintaining some doubt but with an open mind, which is all I can ask of anyone reading this. A cynic is someone with no doubt and a closed mind, very different attitudes indeed.

Miraculous Help

There was a time when I didn't understand, that everything we consider our reality is nothing more than an illusion of our perception. It was causing some confusion in my work, and in what some of the verses of the Bible were trying to say. I was feeling an overall lack of confidence in being able to complete this monumental task, getting caught up in the twisted version of the words I had been taught in Sunday school and feeling incapable of overcoming that hurdle.

This was the status of my work over a period of a couple weeks, when I was invited to another Cyndy party. I welcomed the chance to get some insight through that means, since direct answers from Spirit weren't helping. I don't remember the exact question I asked this time, but the answer is still very clear in my mind. Cyndy told me, "You will understand when you read 3 books".

I asked her if the books were together in one book, because I was thinking they were books of Bible. There I go assuming again. Her answer seemed to surprise her, when she said, "yes, actually, they are now in one book, but they used to be separate books." I don't know why I didn't just ask if they were books in the Bible, except to keep my work unknown by the other guests, so I just chose to assume I knew what she was talking about. I thought I knew exactly what to do, read the Bible more thoroughly.

I tried everything I could think of to differentiate which 3 books of the Bible were going to clarify things for me. It was all the same mass of confusion I'd been struggling with, so I remained just as lost as I had been. Finally, I threw up my hands one day, and said out loud to Spirit, "I give up, Spirit. If you want me to find those 3 books, then you are going to have to put them right in front of me". I was still thinking they were books in the Bible, but I was done looking for which ones. I just left it at that, and continued going through the motions of trying to write the book, and keeping my craft business going, and overall living.

There used to be a place on the Kryon website where you could leave your email address so other people of like mind in your area could contact you. I would occasionally get an email that would lead to a brief conversation via email, but it never amounted to organizing a meeting in person. It was less than a week following my surrender to Spirit for those 3 books, when one email did lead to us agreeing to discuss our mutual interests in person. It was on the first meeting, which involved over 8 hours in a coffee shop, and about 6 hours into that discussion, when she brought up a book she had that she thought I should read.

She said it was given to her by a psychic lady, who told her it wasn't meant for her to read, that she wouldn't understand what it had to say. Her interest in the metaphysical was based more in what happened in our very distant past with some war between the planets and such, something way over my head at the time. So, it made sense that this book wasn't for her, since it talked more of our earthly reality, where my interest lied.

The psychic lady went on to tell her, that she would meet someone someday who she should give it to, and she would know who this person was when she met them. I was that person. She said she tried to read a little of it, and it made no sense to her, so she knew she had to follow through with her instructions.

Wow, okay, I'm guessing you can surmise the first place my thoughts went at this news. I asked her if it was possible it was ever 3 books. She said, "I think it was, actually, because there are 3 separate parts to it". She'd also heard it used to be 3 separate books, and in fact, it had been. We met up a 2nd time, mostly so she could give me the book, and had lunch. It turns out, she was about to move to another part of the country permanently, so I would never have the opportunity to see this lady again.

Are you starting to see how Spirit works? A psychic gives a book to a person and tells her to pass it on to someone she will just "know" is the right person for the book. Another psychic tells me years later that I need to read a book that used to be 3 books. Then Spirit lines her and I up through our mutual interests in the metaphysical. With that in place, Spirit then gives her the instinctive message that I am the person who needs the book and gives me the gut feeling that the book she had was the 3 books I was meant to read. This lady had this book in her possession for years, so this didn't just fall into place in a week or two. Also remember, that lady left town permanently within weeks of our first meeting, so it was a very small time frame this could fit into.

Four people in touch with the forces around them made magic happen for one. That is what I would consider a miracle, but really, it's only an example of how we get help from supernatural sources at times, in fact, often. It's definitely outside the natural laws of our physical world, however, so by definition, this was a miracle. We shouldn't be so arrogant as to assume we know all there is to know about the science of our reality.

It's astounding, when you think about it. Spirit is constantly busy lining things up for us to have our needs fall into place. The sad thing is; most of us miss the signs and opportunities, as they go about thinking their life is all about them. As this book that used to be 3 books will tell you, the population of the entire world is INSANE, and as a result of the insanity, we live in chaos and calamity, wars and disease. As this book will also tell you, and as I am also here to tell the world, yet in a different way with new information, is that LOVE is the answer, the way to manipulate the illusion to your liking.

In case you haven't already guessed it, the book that used to be 3 books is called, A Course In Miracles. It is a channeled book from Spirit, and if you can grasp this, it appears that Spirit is the Spirit of Jesus himself. Even though he never introduces himself as such in the book, he talks about his time on earth and some of the things Jesus did as things he did. So, believe it or not, it's up to you and your ability to accept this biblical thing called "channeling".

Regardless of what you believe, however, I highly recommend reading this book, that is, if you are ready to understand the world around you better, since it can do nothing but help you "overcome the world", as Jesus put it. If interested, you can get the book online at their site, www.acim.org. One of its parts, the 2nd part and easily the largest part in the book, is literally a course you take, one lesson a day for a full year. In the end, it helps you see what I mean when I say, that NOTHING is as it seems.

My Snow Miracle
This is a story of what I consider to be the most important miracle to ever happen to me. It's what I think

about every time I wonder why I'm still sitting here writing, still waiting for the help to come, for my spiritual life to begin as I suffer alone in this world. It's also the last spiritual experience I have to tell you. It may seem small in comparison to some of the other phenomenon I've witnessed, but to me it's huge, because it's what keeps me focused on my path even to this day.

First, I should tell you, I'd finished the first version of my Bible study book within only about 6-8 months from when I first started writing it. As "luck" would have it, that is also when my brother, who I was writing the book for, remember, decided to come live with us for a couple months. Of course, it was also the perfect opportunity for him to read the book I'd written for him. Spirit, I'm sure, had something to do with that timing as well.

It was Steve who first brought it up, but I also felt I was being shown by Spirit, that I should go visit my other brother, Gary, for Thanksgiving. This was actually a pretty tall order, since Gary lived in the deep woods of the far northern part of Montana near Glacier National Park, so winter came pretty early to his house. Looking back, the fact that there would likely be snow on the ground in Montana didn't falter me one bit, and you know how I feel about driving in snow. I just put out a quick prayer to keep the weather nice, and didn't give the timing of that request a second thought. I just figured Spirit was sending me there, so no other consideration was necessary.

Sure enough, it turned out to be one of the driest Novembers on record, and Gary was actually starting to worry about their lack of snow by the time we got there. He said they usually have over a foot on the ground by that time of year, and they hadn't had any snow at all yet. I smiled to myself, realizing just how tall an order that little prayer for clear weather was. That alone was a miracle, but not the miracle this story is about.

It was a wonderful Thanksgiving, one of the best I'd ever had with both of my brothers there. I enjoyed getting to know my older brother's children for the first time, since they were very little toddlers when we'd last seen them. After living in Australia for 8 years, we still had not been up to see him since we'd been back from Australia, so this was quite a treat. I hadn't seen my oldest brother in something close to 12 years or so by then.

My husband and I figured we were pushing our luck to stick around after Thanksgiving, so we were planning on starting the long drive back Friday morning. Gary, was enjoying our stay so much, that he asked if we could stay until Saturday. I also wanted to stay, but really did not want to be caught in snow. Without having an answer for him yet, I retreated to his bathroom and sat down to have a talk with Spirit. I put out the question of whether we could beat the snow if we stayed until Saturday. This is the response I got from Spirit, "you will know when you see the snow".

Oh great, thanks heaps! It seemed to me it would be a bit late by then. So, that part of the message confused me, but then I also got a reassurance from Spirit, as the message continued, "There will not be any snow in the passes when you travel through." That was good news, but I was still wondering what we should do, stay until Saturday or leave Friday morning.

When I came out of the bathroom, my brother's wife was on the computer looking up the weather reports. I went over to her and looked over her shoulder. She was having a hard time finding where to go on the internet for the correct information specific to their remote area. Then I saw it, and I just knew in my heart it was the SNOW Spirit told me to look for in the message. It was a cute little snow icon on the screen, a link with no words or inclination of where it would take you. I told her to click on that snow icon, she did, and presto, we were right where we needed to be to find out that snow was not predicted until late Saturday afternoon.

Sure enough, Spirit was right, I did know when I saw the snow, the snow icon, that is. I decided it was the sign Spirit promised, and that we could stay until Saturday morning, especially since I was also promised by Spirit that there wouldn't be any snow in the mountain passes when I traveled through them, which are the most treacherous areas to drive by far.

The weather held, and Friday was another wonderful day, making the trip one of the best times I've ever spent with my older brother and his family, and even with the treat that my other brother was also there. We headed out Saturday in the late morning (I'm just a late person), with the roads as clear as on any beautiful sunny day. Completely dry, perfect all the way through 2 of the 3 mountain passes we had to drive through.

Since we got such a late start, we decided to stop for the night just before the 3rd pass. I guess I was feeling pretty cocky with my promise from Spirit, really pushing my luck with this one. But, we knew there were no towns on the other side of the last pass where we could sleep, so it was either stop now or we had a very long drive still ahead of us.

Sure enough, the weather reports were on schedule, and we woke up to over a foot of snow on top of our van, not to mention the huge snow drifts all over the place. To make matters worse, it was still snowing and even blowing hard as well. We were in the middle of a snow storm! Now what? We had to keep going because winter had arrived, and it was only going to get worse, so we decided to give it a try.

We got in the van and headed towards the pass, but as we started out, the weather got much worse. Now we were on the highway heading toward the pass with the weather so bad we were the only vehicle on the road. We were only able to drive about 25 mph at best; hardly able to even see the road through what was now a massive blizzard.

I really started having some serious doubts about that promise that there would be no snow in the passes from Spirit. Here we are in a horrible blizzard with snow everywhere heading straight for the last pass! Have I been wrong about the messages I thought I was hearing from Spirit all along? My husband and I decided we would have to give it up and were now looking for the first exit out of this mess. I was really upset by this broken promise from Spirit, and decided it must mean that I have been WRONG all along. I must be imagining all those communications from Spirit!

I was so sure, that if this promise from Spirit didn't come through for me, then everything I believed I was experiencing must be wrong, and I was DONE being wrong. As my husband drove very slowly, I turned my head away from him with tears in my eyes. As I looked out at the snow I said to myself, in fact, I vowed to myself, that if we really are turning back because snow WAS in the last pass, then I am giving up all this "spiritual stuff" forever. I swore to myself, that I will not write the book, and I will never pray to or listen to Spirit again. "It's over", I said to myself, and I meant it with all my being. My life would no longer belong to Spirit!

It was less than a minute later, when suddenly the world changed right before our eyes. The wind stopped blowing, it was no longer snowing, the sun was brightly shining, and this is the real mind blower... the road was COMPLETELY DRY. I'll never forget what I saw that day, a full blown miracle. I looked over my shoulder at the 4 lanes of highway as our car passed from a completely white road to a completely dry black top road, and there was a PERFECTLY STRAIGHT LINE of white and then black all the way across all 4 lanes of the road!!

It must have been bump of snow we crossed over, even though I don't remember feeling a bump. One thing is sure, that the snow stopped completely in one spot to draw a perfect line across the highway, something completely impossible in the world as we know it. Then, to top it off, we discovered we were only about a mile from the pass!!! Turns out, there weren't any more exits before the pass, we had to keep going forward, but it didn't matter now, because Spirit came through on his promise.

As I am sitting here writing this, I am crying my eyes out, because it was a miracle well and true, and because I wouldn't be here writing this if it weren't for that miracle, and because my older brother died of cancer only a month ago (from when I first wrote this). Spirit sent me to spend that last quality time with my older brother and his family, a time I will cherish for the rest of my life.

The irony is, Spirit also made sure I would follow through with my promise, to write this book, by delivering me a miracle I will never forget. Each and every time since then, whenever any doubt would try to creep into my psyche, my thoughts would go back to this day when I almost threw away my promise to deliver the information I was shown to the world forever. It was proof that this is real, that all that has happened to me was for a reason, and that I can't possibly give up on my promise after Spirit delivered so beautifully on his.

The Journey Of Writing

After my snow miracle, I spent the next 10+ years writing and waiting, never doubting my spiritual calling to write a book. I couldn't even tell you how many times I thought the book was finished, and yet, the promised vision never came to release me from the pact. So, I would work harder, and dive deeper into the Bible, and even borrowed a gem book from a friend to painstakingly associate the gems from the Bible to their meanings.

I remember one time I thought for sure the book was done, but thought maybe the vision needed help in the form of meditation. I sat at the picnic table for what must have been hours meditating and waiting for my vision to come. It never came, and neither did any sort of connection to Spirit that day. I had to accept once again, my book must not be done, but still, I never doubted my spiritual calling. I knew absolutely, I am supposed to write a book, now books, so I can share the information I was shown with the world.

The problem with all those pages I'd been writing, however, is they went far beyond that calling. I never noticed it, but my book was no longer about the information I promised to share, even though I always made sure it was buried in there somewhere. Rather, my book predominately became more about the many other spiritual insights I was waking up to at the same time all this writing and researching was going on.

I learned so much in those first 10 years, that I couldn't possibly list it all. It was a process of reading the Kryon books, and then assimilating his message with the message from the Bible, parceled along with the teachings from other sources like my Indian Grandmother and the 3 books condensed to 1 book, which all, of course, had to coincide with the absolute truths I was shown in the all-knowingness.

That is one important aspect of the experience I had in the Grand Canyon. It gave me some very strong absolutes, meaning information I was positively sure were the absolute reality of mankind. With that solid base supporting me, I was able to sort through all the confusion haunting the rest of the population providing me with some real answers to the big questions.

That entire period in my life of learning and writing and researching and writing some more was all very exciting and even mind boggling at times. But as the mysteries were solved, the need for answers began to cease. When my Indian Grandmother died, it felt like I was left on my own to spiritually sink or swim. I stopped trying to connect to Spirit on a daily basis, since unfortunately I was taking that connection for granted by now, and since I didn't have any questions to ask Spirit very often.

I continued writing, but then even that came to an end, as I thought I'd done all I could to perfect that now huge book I'd been writing for over a decade. I sent it off to my husband's sister, since she was the only one patient enough to try to read it to give me some feedback. It was actually the 2nd time I'd sent her a "finished" version, thinking my fixes would make it easier to read. She'd spent nearly 6 months trying to get through half of the first one I'd sent her, so on this 2nd "finished" version, hearing how she was struggling through chapter after chapter, I started to feel sorry for her. After 3 months into it, I told her to send it back to me, because I knew this book was not "finished" either.

Obviously, if the book is that difficult to read, it's not going to be something people will read. It was just too much of a Bible study rather than a book. Worse yet, it was the kind of Bible study nobody studying the Bible would be ready to hear. That's when I knew, the book I'd been writing for 12 years was never going to be published, at least not as it had been written.

I remember, early on in my writing, being worried about compiling enough pages for a decent sized book, when I received a message from Spirit to not worry about the number of pages. By the time I had to give up on the book to nowhere, I had written so much information, that the final work itself covered nearly 400 full 8 1/2"x11" pages, which equates to about 800 pages in normal book sized pages.

Also, due to its overgrown size, I had already divided the work twice, removing another 300 pages or more to be published at a later date in separate books. Clearly, I have a lot to say, so much, in fact, that I don't know if I will live long enough to say it all. Even if all that effort was only to help me learn what to teach that one little girl who is supposed to come to me some day, it was worth it. Everything happens for a reason, even if we can never figure out what that reason is, and even if it causes great suffering. I'm about to give you a huge example of why I say this, a story of a different sort, where spiritual guidance left me and without it I was brought to my knees, and then to death's door.

A Turn For The Worst

With the realization that the book to nowhere was never going to be published as it was written, I had to put away the research materials and let it go without any idea of what to do with the information I'd spent so many years learning. There were other things already filling up my time and consciousness by now anyway, so writing any book was put to the back of my mind. I'd stopped accepting orders from my business as well, so I could spend more quality time with my husband as his health took a bad turn.

From the day he came home early announcing he had been fired from his job, my husband's natural zest for life faded dramatically, and his health quickly followed. It was a very difficult time for both of us, but in different ways and for different reasons. For my husband, the loss of his job made the strong provider part of him feel useless. Worse yet, with so much time on his hands, his memories of the war were now free to haunt him constantly.

It was difficult for me, because I didn't know what to do to help him, or even what was actually wrong with him, since the V.A. doctors weren't giving us any real answers. I knew he had various "war related" conditions, but I didn't understand what he was going through, and he wouldn't share it with me. I would only get hints here and there out of necessity, like when I tried to help him get up once after a fall. He stopped me saying the dizziness hadn't passed yet and he would just fall again if I helped him right then. That was the first time I realized he was even having dizzy spells. No wonder he was falling down all the time. The doctors were blaming the alcohol, but I had my doubts.

Finally, it was one of his falls that killed him, bursting a blood vessel in his brain giving him a hemorrhagic stroke. Bottom line, the doctors, all of them, even the ones in the ICU at the "regular" hospital, did him wrong in every way they could, from lies to mistreatment or no treatment. Even though it made me very angry at the time, I've forgiven all of them now, because at least his suffering is over. He wanted to leave this world, because his painful memories were just too great to endure. I finally get it.

It took a comment from his V.A. counselor for me to truly grasp the extent of his suffering. He told me that most men who had served the type of duty for as long as my husband had, as a combat medic for 3 terms in Vietnam, end up insane in institutions. That also confirmed for me just how strong my husband truly was. He'd done well holding down only 6 jobs throughout his entire career and maintaining a "normal" life, as he remained loyal and true to his one and only wife of 36 years, me. ☺

All those things were reason for them to lessen his PTSD diagnosis, because most men have trouble living a normal existence, but they didn't understand the kind of strength my husband had. For 3 years during the war, and for some 45 years since the war, my husband lived a hero's effort throughout his life. Well done, my dearest loved one! The world needs more heroes like you.

Just so you know, the military did reward his efforts with 2 Bronze Stars, 1 Silver Star and 6 Purple Hearts among the many other medals and promotions he received during his service to our country. My husband really was a hero in every sense of the word, even though he never would accept that honor. He would always tell me that he was just doing his job. That, in my mind, is the mark of a true hero.

Misunderstood Blessings

In all these years, ever since I turned my life over to Spirit, I felt sure Spirit was taking care of me. Even though I was really bad at keeping a watch on the gauges, for example, I never ran out of gas, and I never had a flat tire. My husband didn't know what to make of it sometimes, while I just always felt sure it was Spirit keeping me safe. It unnerved him when something would happen, like the numerous times he ran out of gas just backing out of the driveway when he was only trying to go get some gas in my van for me. That's how close I would come to running out of gas, and yet I never did, running on fumes and a prayer often.

I remember one day, when my husband came running into my office really upset. He suddenly came running into my office to demand some answers. "Can you explain to me how you drove your van with a 6 inch slash in the side of your tire?", he said as he held his fingers 6-7 inches apart to illustrate his point. I'd just returned from one of my long trips to visit with my Indian Grandmother, and it was this kind of thing that really worried him over my safety. All I could do is smile at him, as I shrugged my shoulders and reminded him once again, "I told you, Spirit takes care of me."

It was like that with everything that happened in my life. Finding this land I now reside on in gratitude and the excellent mobile home I bought sight unseen are further examples of how Spirit just seemed to be lining things up just right for me. Everything seemed blessed and Spirit sent, and I remained grateful for Spirit, but I didn't really understand why I was so blessed.

I assumed it was because Spirit wanted me to do this work I was here to do, to write the book to nowhere. I thought I was being kept comfortable so I could do the work without interruption. I knew intellectually that my job on this earth is no greater or more important than anyone else's job, but it was the only reason I could think of for having such a blessed life.

It surprises me, looking back at this, how ignorant I'd been in my understanding of these things, especially after what I was shown in the Grand Canyon. This illustrates how difficult it really was to translate the truth I was shown in the spiritual realm into how that manifests in the physical realm. I had a clear memory of what I'd been witness to, but I didn't understand how to achieve it from the physical perspective.

I knew absolutely, from my experience in the all-knowingness, that Love makes all our problems go away. But, I didn't think I was doing anything in particular to express that Love myself, since I wasn't helping anyone directly. I thought I would have to publish my book before the Love I was feeling towards humanity would do any good for anyone, including me.

What I didn't recognize, is that I had been expressing the Love that makes all our problems go away from the moment I turned my life over to Spirit. I wasn't following Spirit for my sake. I did it only for my Love of Spirit and my Love towards all of mankind, the same Love I felt from within the spiritual realm. My life was blessed because of my intentions of Love.

In other words, it's about what your consciousness is focused on, what your intentions are, where your head is at. It doesn't need to be what you are expressing externally. You can be angry at someone and still Love them. It's about what the motives behind your thoughts and actions truly are. Is it about your Love towards others, or is it about you?

I guess I just hadn't been through enough sorrows yet to figure all this out. Ironically, I thought Spirit was taking care of me so I could complete my work, while all along I couldn't complete my work because I still thought that. The lesson in all this is truly astounding, which is why I have to tell you what happened next, after I lost my husband.

A Handicapped Widow

I'm about to take you on a very different journey, one that's not so blessed and is far from what would be considered a spiritual experience. Keep in mind, as you read this story, that everything really does happen for a reason. The thing to remember, is I'd closed my business over a year before, I was no longer writing any book with little hope or thought of ever writing again, and I'd just lost the one and only true Love of my life. What is most important to notice here, is the Love I'd felt for humanity escaped me temporarily, as I wallowed in grief over my own personal loss.

Due to the solitude my handicap caused, I have no friends or family members living in any nearby state, so I had no support structure in place at all. I was suddenly a handicapped widow completely alone in the world. From the very moment my husband went into the hospital, where he died 5 days later, I felt more alone than ever in my life, and that reality is much worse than I could have ever imagined.

In fact, my own ability to survive was in question, but survival was the least of my worries. I would have welcomed death, but I thought I had to continue, because of my work for humanity. I was still waiting for the vision to release me from the pact so I could fulfill my spiritual promise to share what I was shown with the world. I was still waiting for the promise of help to lose weight to come. I was still holding on to a hope that I still had a spiritual life ahead of me and spiritual success to achieve.

I tried to remain brave, thinking the only hardship I was facing was being alone with my handicap. I assumed Spirit was still going to take care of me. But, from that moment of my husband's final journey forward, the corruption and betrayal of the world took its place in my life. I was now the most vulnerable target for the con-artist possible, a handicapped widow with no children, no family or even friends to come to her defense.

The Abuse Begins

It started with the handyman we had working for us at the time, who seemed to change gears as they carried my husband in the gurney to the ambulance. His intention was to become indispensable as he stepped up to play the man's role while he helped himself to our belongings. He was not only a thief and a liar, but a big time manipulator, evidenced by his repeated efforts to control my mobility by keeping my electric wheelchair broken down for over 3 weeks. He knew I was literally brain dead with grief and, without family or friends to come to my rescue, he was going to take full advantage of every minute of my delirium.

A Turn For The Worst

When it came to my attention that the roof on the rental house was in very bad condition, our coning handyman thought he'd let his friend of 30 years in on this easy mark, a so-called professional roofer. I'm actually glad he did, because it was the roofer's blatant corruption that started to feel like the slap on the face I needed to wake me up to what was going on around me. Realizing that he was such a long term friend of my handyman gave me the presence of mind to pay attention to the con job I was allowing to rule my life. I started to take notice of all I had already lost in my blindness.

Getting rid of that handyman and the problems he introduced, even though very disheartening, seems small compared to what started next. Understand, as you read this horrific story, that I am only skimming over the worst of it. The actual day to day reality was much worse than I could ever put into writing.

Within days of thinking my problems were behind me, I received a phone call from my tenant of 8 years giving me his 30 day notice! I'd spoken to him only a couple weeks prior to confirm his plans before I put any money into fixing that roof. He had assured me he planned to stay there at least another couple of years. So, now I'm getting lied to by the man who brought his children to my husband's funeral!

My husband and I had really trusted that man and his family, as we watched his two children grow up over those 8 years of living next door. We believed him when he said he was taking care of the chimney on a yearly basis, for example, when we offered to send someone over. According to our chimney man, who inspected it afterwards, he had never had the chimney cleaned in the entire 8 years, and there had been at least 3 chimney fires evidenced by the 4 broken ceramic tiles, so now the fireplace is completely unburnable.

In reality, what I was facing in the house they vacated placed the chimney as the least of my problems. Among the worst of the problems was a leak in the water heater, which was allowed to continue for YEARS. The floor was so rotted from water damage, that there were massive holes going all the way through 4 layers of flooring, totaling 2 inches thick, to the outdoors!! He had simply placed pieces of plywood over the holes so they could walk on it. By the time the demolition of the floor was done, so a new floor could be laid, the entire kitchen floor and half the laundry room floor was completely rotten through. Talk about neglect!! He had literally lived there until it was no longer livable.

To make matters seem 10 times worse, I was now living with NO INCOME what-so-ever. As soon as my husband died, the VA benefits stopped, and that along with the rental income was all the income we had. I was now living off of our meek savings alone. We'd never gotten around to establishing a proper retirement fund, and the only life insurance I had any hope of receiving was a small policy the VA provided, but that would depend on whether they decided he died from war related illnesses or not. Is a stroke war related?

The thing that made this a huge issue, is even after 5 months the death certificate was still not being finalized, and only then because I went to the media for help in exposing their neglect and ended up as front page news!! It was several more months before I got the small insurance payment, all of which, and even more, has now been swallowed up in the rental home repairs and the mortgage I was paying for an empty house.

A Turn For The Worst

    I seem to be painting a pretty rough picture of my life right now, I know. But in truth, it was a whole lot worse, and I've barely scratched the surface of what was yet to come. At this point, I'm only about 5-6 months into the grief over losing the deepest Love I've ever known. I still had a long way to go.

    They say, it takes about 6 months to get over the loss of a loved one, but I disagree. I'd have to say that you never "get over it", because Love never dies. As far as how long it takes to stop crying every day, it depends on how deep that Love is, and on how important it is that you get on with your life. Kids, for example, are a big driving force to get you out of your stupor of grief. However, I don't have any kids, and nobody else providing support to help me overcome my despair.

    There was only one reason for me to get on with my life, which was to fix that house and recover that lost income, and only then so I could continue to wait for those spiritual promises. While I was in the depths of my grief through these several months of turmoil, I knew deep down inside, that there had to be a reason for it. Spirit couldn't really be abandoning me, could he? That knowing was so buried by the overwhelming disaster confronting me; that hope was having a difficult time surviving as things went from bad to worse.

    The next player in this saga had been coming twice a month to work as a maid, having started shortly after my husband died. Her business included house repairs with the help of her mate. Her thing was to live in houses rent free while she repaired them. When my dilemma began, having no friends or family to turn to, it really was the obvious choice to hire her to do the repairs on the rental house while she lived there.

Even though she seemed to be the obvious solution to my dilemma, I was feeling very leery of her due to the situation with her current landlord. She was complaining about the horrendous things he was doing like shutting off the utilities, which I could only surmise was designed to try to force her to move out. Having young children, I knew it would be difficult to get her out once she moved in, and there was no way she could afford my price for rent. It wasn't long before my initial concerns started proving themselves correct and I had to get rid of her before I couldn't get rid of her.

By that time the house was 10 times worse, because she had gone through demolishing things to force me to fix them to her liking. The place was such a wreck at this point, that it scared most of the handymen I tried to hire away. Finally, I hired the #1 A-Rated listing from an online site to do the job, which is when my troubles went from bad to a whole lot worse. He quickly realized that this was as easy a mark as it gets, since my handicap made it impossible for me to even enter the house, so, nobody was overseeing his work. All he had to do is stage some photos of the progress, and he got paid for the phase he had supposedly finished.

After 3 weeks of this, I pointed out that the job was going much slower than he had promised. I ended up firing him due to undependability. All I can say is THANK GOD I did, because, this is the stage of this fiasco where things got down right INSANE. The amount of out and out vandalism is way too long to list here, so I will only hit the highlights to give you an overall picture of how horribly this disaster had gone so wrong.

I hired my new maid's husband, who brought in a team of 5 workers. The first thing they had to do is clean up the mess that last guy left behind, including the heater vents the jerk had used as trash receptacles. He'd left the bathroom window wide OPEN when he buried it behind the new tub surround, which was only discovered because he had installed it crooked and even cut into the wood beams to force it in place.

As bad as all that was, it barely touches the depth of destruction left behind by that obviously self-proclaimed #1 contractor. Even though I had purchased rolls and rolls of masking tape and masking paper, not one roll was used. He made no effort of any sort to prep the job before walking in there with a paint sprayer.

He'd mixed all the various types and colors of paint I'd chosen together to create one horrible color, and just started spraying paint everywhere, and I mean everywhere! The appliances, light fixtures, windows, sinks, faucets, cabinets, built in wood grain book cases, wood grain fireplace mantel, custom painted wood grain front door, all other doors, door knobs, hinges, EVERYTHING was painted with heavy overspray.

Just revisiting this long process of corruption and betrayal to tell you this story is difficult, but living it was nothing short of complete and total devastation. All I could do is sleep and cry for days on end, because now these new guys were playing games too. Even as they stroked my back and told me what "good Christians" they were and how bad they felt for my ordeal, my instincts were screaming at me that they were not who they were pretending to be. At a cost of $3000 per week they were acting like they were doing me a favor.

The first thing I told them I needed, for example, was to have a railing installed on the stairway to the porch so that I could get in to see the place. That didn't happen, even though I repeatedly asked why it wasn't happening. The response was always that they would get right on that, but they never did. It quickly became obvious that they didn't want me to have access to the house, because they also wanted to nurse this easy mark all the way to the bank. But at this point, what choice did I have? It's not like there is anybody out there willing to do a fair job for fair pay. I was beyond hope for that.

It was 4 weeks into their work, now already beyond the date when they promised I could have a renter move in, when in one of the photos I saw a strange line on the floor, which turned out to be grout between tiles that didn't line up. All I can figure is he was conserving tile so he could steal what was left and use it on another job. Regardless, when I saw that, I was appalled!!! He was swearing to me it was the only way the job could have been done. I simply am not that stupid and neither was he.

This was a Friday night, and all I could do is try my brother once again. Crying my eyes out, I pleaded for his help. Finally, he agreed to come to my aid, and by Monday morning he was here proving what I had been suspecting. They were dragging out the job as long as they could, and billing me for time they didn't even work. The biggest mistake I made with them is agreeing to pay them by the hour, but with the mess the house was in, I thought it was the only way I could have gotten anyone to do the job.

It took another week and a half under my brother's strict supervision for them to get their act together and finish the job with another week's worth of work my brother had to complete on his own just to make the house rentable. After spending well over $45,000 for a job that should have only cost $12,000, that house should have been shining like a brand new mansion, far from their end result. The outside and chimney were never even touched, and the work they did was very unprofessional.

Rock Bottom

That's where I was, the lowest I've ever been in my life at this point. Still grieving the loss of my husband, I was now devastated by the scum of the earth feeling entitled to what little I had left in the world. I achingly searched my soul, wondering why all this had to happen at once. I was looking for the lesson in this, where any reason would have sufficed, but no answers came.

With my brother gone and the rental house empty, all I could do is cry and sleep, since now the grieving could finally begin. Overwhelmed by depression, loneliness and helplessness, I wondered why Spirit had deserted me in my hour of need. Reviewing my life, I knew deep down at the root of my soul that all those amazing spiritual experiences, messages and miracles could NOT possibly have all been for nothing. Still, my hope for ever realizing a spiritual destiny was dying rapidly. Feeling betrayed by Spirit for the many promises never coming true, life did not seem worth the effort, and in truth, it was becoming very apparent that it wasn't even a sustainable possibility.

With little hope left, I made a pact with myself on the 1st year anniversary of my husband's death. I vowed that one year from that date I would join him if the spiritual purpose I thought was my destiny had not materialized by then. I was giving it one more year to try once again to get my message out to the world by starting over in my writing effort. If that vision never came during my proposed last year of life, then I would leave my work with my sister-in-law to publish after I was gone, since she wouldn't be bound by a pact. I figured, one way or another, my information would find its way to the masses, if I could just write it in a way that could be received by people.

This is where my thoughts were taking me when I first sat down to write this book you are reading, starting over from scratch. Since so much has happened to me in the month of April, I realized my vision could also come in April, which meant I would have to hold on 4 days beyond the anniversary of my husband's death, since he died on April 26th. By the time I reached that date, however, hope was already pretty far gone.

Needless to say, severe depression was setting in fast and furious by the first week of May. I was constantly considering suicide and crying on a daily basis. My biggest concern was whether I would have the courage to pull the trigger or even know how to use the gun I had waiting for me in the drawer. As I worked at trying to complete my book, I was praying daily for Spirit to either send me death or send me the promises I'd been waiting for.

Facing Death

It was less than a month after the 2nd anniversary of my husband's death that my health took a devastating turn for the worse. This has been a very long and miserable ordeal, so again, I will try to limit the details to something bearable to read. Just know once again that what I've been going through over more than a year now has been far worse than the pain and agony any words can describe.

My ability to catch my breath was the first thing to go, decreasing more every day causing my immobility to be multiplied substantially with every gasp for breath. Then suddenly, even overnight it seemed, my body swelled up to the point that I felt like a huge blowfish barely able to move at all. As my joints ached more and more, I took excessive amounts of Motrin, which I came to believe was why I started bleeding internally.

At some point early into this, I'd scraped the side of my lower leg on the foot rest of my wheelchair. It created a minor sore, not even skin deep, and yet it started to leak a clear liquid so rapidly it developed a puddle on the foot rest of my wheelchair within minutes after sitting down. My body seemed to be breaking down in every way it could.

Being home bound, going to a doctor was not a solution available to me. As a desperate move, I hired an LPN off Craig's list to help me take care of my leg, since I couldn't even reach it over my swelled belly. She could only come 3 times a week to soak it and wrap it, but her wrap would fall off only hours after she left due to the weight of the constant flow of fluids.

As my physical condition continued to get much worse, in a spiritual way things seemed to change for the better. The LPN was not only able to hear my truth, but seemed to thirst for more. In all these years, I'd never met anyone who could hear me without judging me as crazy or completely misguided. It made carrying this knowledge more of a burden than the gift it was, because it set me up as an outcast from the world. The relief in finally being able to speak openly brought me to tears as she expressed her desire to learn more.

My leg needed daily care, so the LPN recommended a friend of hers who could come every day to change the wrap. This 2nd nurse could also hear my spiritual truth, even if without as much enthusiasm. I was encouraged, thinking that perhaps the world was finally ready to hear me, or maybe I was finally articulating it properly, or both.

The LPN was actually a hospice nurse. Knowing my situation of no family or friends, she said she would help me if and when I made the choice of death. She said she knew people have to be able to make that choice sometimes and she wouldn't want me to suffer through it. She was letting me know she could qualify me for hospice care if I wanted it. It didn't make sense to me at the time, because I figured if I was going to choose death, it would be as quick as a bullet exits a gun. I didn't know what to think, since hospice is what you do when all hope for survival is gone.

I told my daily nurse about her visit, and that's when the weight of my situation really hit me. She told me that what the LPN was offering me was DEATH! She said I had a choice, my daily nurse was offering me life, and the LPN was offering me death. They had mentioned things between them, like "it could go septic at any moment", but that didn't mean a thing to me. I now know that going septic means you only have hours to live, if that. No wonder she was offering me hospice care.

What I didn't understand, and these nurses were trying to tell me, is that I was already choosing death by refusing to go to the hospital. My reaction was always, "are you kidding me? It's a sore on my leg!!!" Problem is, however, fluids had now started to leak out of my other leg, and there was no sore there. Beyond that, it was starting to show signs of being infected.

This may seem strange, but the realization that I was that close to dying was actually a revival of hope for me. It showed me that Spirit had heard my prayers. Spirit was giving me what I had prayed for, and even when I had asked for it to happen, since this all began shortly after the 2nd anniversary of my husband's death. That meant Spirit had NOT deserted me.

As crazy as it may sound, I was relieved to know that my prayers were being answered. After living a life literally directed by Spirit, the feeling of being left on my own following my husband's passing devastated me. I really needed this reassurance that I had not been completely abandoned. I could accept that Spirit couldn't fulfill those promises in my requested time frame, so the only other option was to grant me my request for death. At least I was being heard, even though it wasn't really the outcome I was hoping for.

Choosing Life

For the first time in my life, I had to make the choice between life and death. Could I continue in this horrible existence without my husband and without those promises from Spirit being realized? Could I let go of my hope for a spiritual life and still choose my life of solitude over the death I was now facing? The thought of leaving this place of suffering was very tempting, but this didn't feel right. I hadn't yet completed my work, my promise to Spirit. Even though I'd prayed for death to come, I didn't expect it. I figured if I was going to die, it was going to be by my own hand once my book was finished. Death should not come this way.

What taking my own life would require is a complete loss of hope, which was no longer that far gone thanks to something else that daily nurse said to me only a couple of days prior to this conversation. She didn't realize how important her little comment was, when she simply asked me if I was sure the pact I had with Spirit covered everything I was giving it. As soon as she said that, it hit me like a ton of bricks. WOW!! NO it did NOT!! It only included the controversial parts of the Bible, which I was unsure of at the time. The pact did NOT include what I knew as absolute!

I was the one who had established the rules of that pact, after all, so all I needed to do is think back on what

Vision Of Truth

rules I had laid down. I had asked for that vision when I was upset over the controversial verses I was finding. I wanted a confirmation that I had all THOSE truths completely correct, because if I was going to state them as the truth, then I'd better be right or I'd be risking my life over a misperception. I realized my pact had nothing to do with what I was shown in the Grand Canyon, just for starters, because I had no doubt about that information. I didn't need Spirit to confirm when I had that right, and more importantly, it was never a part of the pact I had made with Spirit.

I realized in that moment, that the many years of waiting could finally be over right there and then. Prior to this, I was still convinced I couldn't publish anything until I'd been released from the pact. All I had to do now is finish the book I had been working on for the past year, and I could publish it freely without delay. I just needed to make sure it only covered the information not bound by the pact, but it was primarily what it still is, a spiritual memoir, so that wasn't a problem.

With my book still incomplete, it wasn't my time to die, so I told the daily nurse that day that I choose life. I'll never forget her response. She said, "You'll have to make that choice over and over again". I didn't really understand her response at the time, but I sure do understand it now. After having to repeatedly choose life over the next year of ups and downs, agony and pain, I realize how difficult coming back from the brink of death can be. In fact, I'm still struggling with my recovery as I write this, but there is an important lesson in it I need to share with you before we move past this.

An aggressive UTI (Urinary Tract Infection), which I apparently had for years, finally landed me in the hospital with a 104 degree fever. During my 11 day stay in the hospital, they told me it was Congestive Heart Failure, among what may be other problems, that caused fluids to swell my body up and the shortness of breath. But everything was fine by the time they informed me, because my heart was now testing within the normal range.

I noticed that my urine was very dark all through the hospital stay, which I knew was a result of kidney problems, but they never had any answers for me when I inquired about it. I'd had my kidneys fail on me years prior when I went to the hospital for heat stroke. It bothered me that these medical professionals didn't seem concerned about my dark urine, but it cleared up on the day I left the hospital, so I let the questions go.

I'd lost more than 130 pounds worth of fluids from the aggressive diuretics they gave me intravenously. My home health nurses now coming on a weekly basis even told me I should buy a new wardrobe because my clothes were hanging like a tent around me and down to the ground almost tripping me. It made me realize that a large portion of the weight I'd been carrying for years was fluids, not fat as even I had assumed.

There were still more fluids that could come off, so the hospital prescribed the highest dosage possible of a drug called Lasix, 160 mg daily, which is far more than a human being can live with. I was going to the bathroom every 10-15 minutes all day long even though I didn't take the full dose prescribed. It was simply too much to bear, since it didn't even allow me time to make meals for myself.

Something Wasn't Right

There was something my Guru said that haunted me from the very start of all these health issues. My life wasn't supposed to go like this according to him, which left me confused but convinced it wouldn't be an ongoing situation. And yet, the home nurses were telling me that my condition was permanent, that there was no cure for Congestive Heart Failure (CHF) and people die from it eventually.

This didn't sit right with me, because for one thing, my Guru told me when and how I will die, which is still a good 20+ years in the future. Even more confusing was that he also said I will not die from any ailment. He said I would die by my own choice, as a knowing that I'd done all I could so it was time to go, but he was not talking about suicide either. He said I wouldn't feel death, that I would just lay down and leave this world. I asked him if he meant I would die in my sleep of old age. His response was, "that is what others will think, but you will just choose to go".

I didn't understand what he meant at the time, but I think I do now. If I am right then it will require the spiritual success he promised in every sense of the word to achieve it. I'll need the next 20 years to reach that high level of awakening. If my Guru was right, then this thing these medical professionals were telling me is going to kill me should not be happening to me. Of course, I had to keep my confusion entirely to myself, since they would have no interest in a Guru's message.

There was even more to what my Guru told me that conflicted directly with what these professionals were telling me was wrong with me. He also told me was that I would never contract ANY disease as long as I live. Oh sure, he had already warned me of the mobility issues I would have, but having the knowledge that I would NEVER have a disease was so comforting to me you can't imagine.

I used to worry about that kind of thing because of my distaste for all those healthy foods everyone tells me I should be eating. I assumed at the time that my Guru told me this so I could stop worrying. Now I understand there was another very important reason. Because, if I could trust his information, then I wouldn't fall victim to the doctors assumptions.

Up to this point it was the case too, I was as healthy as any thin person before all this started happening. Not only is someone weighing 450 pounds not a diabetic, but I also do NOT have high blood pressure. Every doctor I went to for a thyroid test was convinced that I should have diabetes. They would take my money to give me a diabetes test INSTEAD of the thyroid test I thought I was paying for, leaving me with no thyroid results. I can't count how many times I was given a diabetes test, and every time I PASSED. The hospital even tried to feed me diabetic food ignoring that I'd passed their test, "just in case". I'm obese, therefore I must be a diabetic!!! It's infuriating!!

This is only a small part of why I have a distrust for doctors. They want to force me to fit in the box they have with the label on it. If I'm not going to fit in their box, then they want nothing to do with me. That's why going to the hospital when all these problems started was the last thing I wanted to do, because I knew they would get it wrong too. But when they came up with such a horrible sounding diagnosis with the proof of fluids coming off me, I felt I had to believe them.

All through this, I just quietly knew my life was not supposed to be going like this. I can't be having a disease, and yet CHF sure did sound like a disease to me. Although I was testing normal when I left the hospital, the Guru had told me I would never contract ANY disease, even briefly. And now the home health nurses are telling me I would suffer from it for the rest of my life? Something must be wrong somewhere. If they were right and my Guru was wrong, then all the spiritual promises must be wrong. It was having a very detrimental effect on my hope once again.

Feeling defeated, I fell in line when the home health nurses convinced my doctor to refill the Lasix prescription the hospital had prescribed. I did my best to prove them wrong convinced this couldn't be the story of the rest of my life. Working very hard through the pain of daily physical therapy to regain my strength, I was starting to see some improvement in my ability to get around. At the same time I noticed the swelling was returning slowly and the pain in my joints was getting a lot worse, along with new pains and muscle cramps that went unexplained.

A trip to the doctor had me convinced the swelling was due to high levels of inflammation discovered in my blood. He set up an appointment with a specialist in arthritis and inflammation, which put me in a 4 month waiting line. In the meantime my physical therapy began going backwards, since my thighs swelled so large they couldn't pass by each other when I tried to walk. The pain worsened substantially and expanded throughout my body. It got so bad that I could even feel my muscles weakening every day as I worked harder doing my exercises to build them up.

My physical therapist seemed to have no mercy for my condition. She placed what were now unattainable goals on my exercise regime threatening the loss of Medicare support if I didn't attain them. Convinced I probably had arthritis and needed to just "man up", she pushed me to the point of tears every time she came. I did my best to meet those goals even in her absence, but still my progress went in reverse as my muscles diminished and my body swelled up more every day.

A Turn For The Worst

      To make a long story short, there came a day when my condition became more than I could bear and I felt sure it would only be a matter of time before my muscles would fail completely. My belly and thighs became so swollen that every movement was an overwhelming struggle I was forced to fight alone. The shortness of breath returned to make the battle to maintain my survival even more difficult. I knew I wouldn't be able to keep up this struggle through the pain and effort much longer.

      It was time to let my hopes for all those spiritual promises go. My Guru must have been wrong, and if he was wrong, that meant all the promises from Spirit were wrong. I had to face it, I had been hoping for an unrealistic pipe dream. Nobody is going to come help me lose the weight as was promised, and I obviously must have some sort of disease causing me overwhelming agony.

      I knew in my heart that I was dying without any help or understanding coming from anyone. I started asking about how hospice works. They said I was far from that, but I knew better. After all, they only saw me an hour a week. They didn't know what I was going through on a daily basis. I felt I knew my condition far better than they did. I was dying in front of their eyes and they didn't even know how close to death I was, because I could feel my muscles dying, and remember, the heart is a muscle. I just knew that when the day came that I couldn't make it to the bathroom, death would follow shortly afterwards.

My Promise Was Fulfilled

      As I was facing death once again, I was comforted by the one thing I had accomplished, I'd finished my book. It was in the first few months after returning from the hospital that I completed it. It's worth noting that during those months of writing my health was improving quickly, even to the point that the nurses were bragging over my astounding reversal from death itself. As I searched for the means of publishing my book, and doing final edits, I must have rewritten the last chapter at least 6 times because of the struggle that had returned. With my book finished, and therefore my focus on Love gone, my health began to decline once again and I needed to be honest with my readers in that final chapter.

Finally, I was able to finish that last chapter with my truth expressed as best as I could. I found a self-publishing company I thought may have been Spirit sent, since it was a company I found somewhat by accident who is solely interested in spiritual or self-help books. Once I'd paid them several thousand dollars more than I'd expected to pay for this kind of service, my health suddenly took a very severe turn for the worst. I was thankful I had been honest with my readers because it didn't look good.

My Last Ultimatum
I really did fight as long as I could, and fought off the depression as well as I could. With my muscles diminishing substantially on a daily basis, it became an overwhelming reality I felt I had to face. The life I thought I was supposed to be living was just not meant to be. I was confused because I thought the refocusing of my consciousness on Love while I finished my book should have turned my life around. And yet, within days of sending it off to a publisher my struggle took a very bad turn for the worst once again.

Sharing what I was shown in the all-knowingness was the only actual promise I had made, and I'd fulfilled it, so at least my life wouldn't be a complete waste. If all those spiritual signs of my predestiny were meant to be, then I shouldn't have been forced into a life of misery. I figured the disposition of my predestiny didn't work out as planned, so Spirit had to give up on me.

On the day I finally came to this realization, I had a talk with Spirit before I gave up on Spirit forever. I was downright angry with Spirit that day, when I said out loud to the air in my living room, "Okay, I'm done. I'm letting the fight go right now. If you want me to live then you better do something about it, because I AM DONE! I simply cannot fight the hopeless battle for this worthless life anymore!!"

I even called my sister-in-law to let her know I was going to find a lawyer to pass my copyright and publishing rights over to her. I figured someone should oversee the progress and reap the benefits, if there were any. She agreed to do what she could. She understood.

I actually felt very relieved after making the decision to give up the fight for survival. It was comforting to know I wasn't going to have to struggle in misery much longer. I just had to hang in there long enough to make sure my book hit the market, since they probably wouldn't have done the work if I weren't here to make them do as they promised with my money.

The book was supposed to reach the market within a couple more months, so it was a very attainable goal to strive for. I figured I would keep up the PT until then, but only to a bearable degree, just so I could try to maintain my ability to make it to the bathroom and keep myself and my animals fed. I felt confident my muscles had a couple more months left in them before they weakened to the point of losing the battle.

It was the very next appointment with my Physical Therapist, which was about 2 days after I'd made this latest ultimatum with Spirit, when something I didn't expect at all happened. I wasn't looking for it, or expecting any help from Spirit. My hope and faith in Spirit was truly gone, so it took a while for me to realize Spirit was clearly behind what happened next.

With no warning, a complete stranger came to my door. She was a contractor who filled in on rare occasions when the home health company was short on physical therapists or nurses. It turns out, my regular PT called in sick for the first time ever, so she was sent in her place at the last minute. Oh well, that was fine with me. It meant I wouldn't have to argue with my regular PT about working so hard, since I had no intention of working myself to the point of agony ever again.

I think I may have mentioned the pain I was in, but that was all I said to her without expanding on the extensive problems I was having or my loss of hope and decision to let the fight for life go. I wasn't even in a sour mood over it, because the decision to let life go was actually a huge relief I was still enjoying.

She seemed to understand my pain like nobody had before. She told me she'd been in this business for 30 years and that she has watched the medical profession go from fair to completely worthless. She said the doctors no longer have any say, that it's all being controlled by the insurance companies and lawyers. I didn't really care about any of that, and just agreed with her, since of course it is true. But, to me, it was Spirit who let me down, not the doctors, at least that was my understanding at this point in time.

It didn't matter anyway. My time was done, my life was over, even though I never said those words to her or anything close. She continued ranting on about it, as she finished taking my vitals. It was time for me to start my exercises, but she was still talking about the failures of the medical industry. I wasn't really listening, since it seemed like something nobody could do anything about.

But, then she did something to get my attention, she got in my face. She actually got down on her knees in front of me, put her hand on my knee, and spoke directly to my face to continue what she was trying to tell me. I could tell it was hurting her to be on her knees like that, but she continued to suffer through it to keep my attention focused on her words.

She was telling me that I am the only one who can fix me, and that I have to be my own advocate. She was saying the doctors are never going to find the solution, since they don't understand what I'm going through and have their hands tied by insurance and their fear of law suits. She told me that everyone has a basket to offer me, but that only one item in their basket will help me. So, I should take from each basket what I know is beneficial and throw all the rest of it away. She said I am the only one who can know what will help me and what won't.

Then she started to repeat over and over that this is my platform. She said it is not time for my life to be over, that I still had something I needed to do. She told me I am here for a reason, and this is my platform to carry out my work. I asked her what she meant by that, and she told me that I am meant to tell people my story and when I do it will help people. But, first I have to make myself better, be my own advocate, and throw away any doctor's orders that are not helping me.

I started to realize this lady must have been sent by Spirit. She did not get up from her knees for most of that hour, constantly looking at me square in the face as she stressed repeatedly that my life is not over and I still had work to do. I was sure I'd never mentioned that I'd given up the fight, or that I'd ever thought I had any purpose to fulfill, so how did she know that? Finally, I heard her, which brought me to tears as I asked her what I could do.

That's when she finally got up from the floor and told me exactly what to do. She said I should get on the computer and look up what will help CHF naturally. She said I don't need the drugs the doctors want to give me. I can do it with alternative medicines. Wow!! This lady is a nurse, in the medical profession for 30 years, and she was telling me to give up on the doctors and look for alternative medicine!!

She swore that if I dared tell anybody that our entire session was this conversation she would deny it. It was her way of asking me to not turn her in for not doing her job of making me exercise. I flat out lied to protect her, and got busy immediately going online to research alternative CHF methods of recovery. I knew in my heart that Spirit had sent her, and held her message close to my heart and focus. That lady saved my life that day.

That is why I know I had to include this part of my story in this book. Because she told me, this is my platform, and that I need to tell people my story so they can learn from it. There is still much to tell.

The Reason For Everything

One thing I want to be sure to express is that all throughout my years of suffering and pain I never faltered in what I know as absolute. What faltered was my faith in my own destiny and in what I had assumed Spirit promised me. I only doubted me, not the realities I was shown while in the all-knowingness. Knowing absolutely that Love is all that matters and that if you Love all that is then all your trouble will fade away, I only wondered what I was doing wrong to meet those laws of the universe. I still had some lessons to learn on how this reality works, which is what the reason for my suffering was all about.

Discovering Solutions

Starting even before that lifesaving angel showed up at my door, it took me several months to learn enough information about my condition to be able to piece together what was wrong with me and the care I was receiving. I got it from researching the internet, as my lifesaver instructed I should, but also from asking the right questions of the various nurses and doctors surrounding me. Rather than bore you with the long process of how I put one small piece next to the other to figure it all out, I will jump to the conclusions I was finally able to reach.

The truly astounding thing to me is how all these medical professionals enjoy keeping secrets. It's as if the patient is the enemy they need to keep in the dark at all cost. They tell just enough to stop the questions and cause you to fall in line with their demands. So, I had to become knowledgeable enough to ask just the right question, so that a single simplified answer would hit the mark, yes or no. In other words, I had to figure it out on my own and then look for confirmation of my analysis.

The first thing I learned came from the internet, where I researched the true meaning of the word, "disease", and how it differs from ailments or "conditions". I was concerned with the promise from my Guru that I would never contract a disease. As it turns out, he was right once again, so far at least. Not only is my thyroid problem a condition in my case, but so is Congestive Heart Failure a condition rather than a disease. The difference, it seems, is when a condition physically changes your body it becomes a disease, like when Cancer alters your cells or when surgery is required.

I learned much later that not only is CHF not a disease that a person is stuck with for life, but it is more the symptom of my true condition rather than the cause. It turns out the heart gets congested by fluids surrounding it, making it difficult to pump properly. That means the fluids built up from somewhere first causing my heart to fail. CHF definitely adds to the problem, but in my case at least, it was not the initial cause of the fluids building up in my body.

There are thousands of people dying every year from CHF, and I was about to join them. This is why it is important that I tell my story. I have to wonder how many are dying from the treatment of a SYMPTOM, and that treatment actually exacerbates the condition!! Worse yet, the treatment is so miserable it takes away a person's desire to live, since nobody is offering a recovery or even any relief from their suffering.

As I explain my situation, understand that I'm only telling you my story, so you would need to do your own research to see if any of it corresponds to your situation or not. I'm not trying to claim my condition is the same for everyone, but only that we all need to learn about what is going on in our own body. We need to stop putting all our hopes of recovery in the hands of the medical industry, because their primary objective is to treat our symptoms, not help us recover from whatever is causing them.

Of course, we've all heard this before, that the doctors only treat the symptoms, but what never occurred to me was that they could actually be worsening the core problem with the drugs they prescribe for the symptoms. In other words, they ARE causing harm, which goes directly against the oath they took as a doctor.

I now understand why the hospital never responded to my inquiries about my kidneys when I noticed the dark urine. It was because the drugs they were giving me were the cause!! Worse yet, they knew I had a kidney problem since it was the same hospital I'd gone to with the heat stroke.

It appears it was my kidneys that were causing the fluids to build up initially as well. It must have started when I had that heat stroke, but I was never told there was damage to my kidneys, only that they had shut down briefly. I didn't find out I had a damaged kidney until years later, when I applied for social security disability. To this day, even though I've literally begged my doctor to review my hospital records and tell me what it means to have a damaged kidney, I've not been told anything more. He refuses to do the research considering it as being in the past. How ridiculous is that?

The further damage they were doing to my kidneys from their diuretic drug, Lasix, was only part of the problem caused by their treatment of a symptom. It turns out it is basic Medication 101 that you MUST always prescribe potassium with a diuretic, especially when prescribing such an aggressive one at the highest dose possible with endless refills. Nobody ever did anything about it, even though several people noticed. I was on that drug for a year before the oversight was remedied. In the meantime, my muscles were starved of crucial nutrients causing me to suffer in misery for more than 6 months of that year with agonizing pain as I did my best to meet the unattainable goals set by my physical therapist.

I finally realized that the excessive exercise being forced onto my starving muscles is what was causing the inflammation, which increased the pain substantially. It was the specialist who informed me that the lack of potassium can even cause paralysis, because the muscles weaken until they finally just shut down completely. That is exactly how I was feeling. I knew my muscles were dying, and now this man is telling me how close I was to total paralysis!!

I was dying right in front of all their eyes, while all the physical therapist and other medical professionals would do is blame me for eating too much salt or not exercising enough. It was their treatment that was the cause of all of my suffering, from the drug that was making my kidney condition worse and my muscles to weaken daily to the excessive exercise taking my muscles to their limit resulting in extreme inflammation.

I was finally able to put two and two together when I asked my doctor for an anti-inflammatory prescription. I was thinking the over the counter one I was doing wasn't helping enough, and thought there had to be something out there that would work. The doctor refused, even though my blood tests showed extreme inflammation levels. When I asked why, I found out they could make the swelling problem worse by causing harm to the kidneys. Eureka!!

You mean damaged kidneys can cause fluids to build up? It was all news to me, and yet all these medical professionals I was surrounded by knew it from day one. I immediately stopped doing ALL drugs and within 3 days my kidneys began working hard at flushing the fluids out of my body all on their own.

The swelling had reached a point where I could barely move again, so my kidneys had a lot of work to do. Without any diuretic I was forced to the bathroom every hour throughout the day AND night. Just so you know, I went online to research CHF as my lifesaver instructed, and I found some supplements that would help me. I initially got something that would help my CHF condition and then something for my weakened muscles and inflammation. However, after spending over $400 on alternatives, the solution helping me the most is avoiding anything that will harm my kidneys.

A Disguised Blessing

As I waited patiently for the new alternatives for my CHF condition to come in the mail, I found out that the self-publishing company I had given thousands of dollars to were FRAUDS!! There was a class action law suit still pending against them for both fraud and for misleading marketing practices. Worse yet, the things they were being sued for were already starting to happen to me.

They were NOT who they said they were, and they had pillaged 10's of 1000's of dollars out of other people. It turns out, that initial money I gave them was only the start of their campaign to swindle me out of more. They got one lady for over $32,000 by telling her the initial payment didn't include the marketing she thought she had already paid for, which is exactly what I thought I had paid for.

You were probably wondering how the book I'd already published could be getting edited now with this new addition, and even how it became a series of books if it was a single book. This is how that happened, because there was something in their contract that bothered me, a clause that gives them rights beyond contract termination. Even though it is probably meant to cover them on books that had already reached the market, it didn't sit right with me.

The discovery that I had invested in a fraudulent company initially appeared to be more trouble than I could bear. It felt like it was some more of the world's corruption coming to haunt me, but it turned out to be a blessing in disguise. Not only was I was able to terminate their contract, but I was even able to get my money back thanks to the help from my credit card company. In fact, no money ever left my bank account, since the credit card bill was barely coming due when I discovered this.

Spirit, I'm sure, had a hand in this raw "luck", because this huge charge should have shown up on the prior bill. I looked for it and expected it to be there. As always, I would have paid it in full if I'd have found it on my bill. Clearly, Spirit caused their charges to be left off my bill long enough for me to discover their intentions. I also feel strongly that Spirit wanted me to make that mistake in choosing the wrong company, since it forced me to change several things about how my book is being written.

Because of that questionable clause I found in their contract, I felt the need to change the name of my book, and even the content to some degree, so that it would not be the same book they had. I'd filed my copyright legally several months prior to giving them a copy, so I know I'm safe there. But, I didn't want them to recognize my final book in case it goes viral by some miracle. It just wasn't worth the risk.

Besides, that book was too big, and that was after removing the equivalent of about 5 chapters, which is where the third book in this series is starting from. I finally recognized that I have way too much to say to try to fit it all into a single book. Plus, I now had to add this story of my health struggle. That lifesaving nurse told me this is my platform, and that I am meant to tell my story to help others, so I had to add that. Now let me clearly state what I have learned from my overwhelming turmoil.

The Law Of Love

Throughout these years of suffering, starting with the loss of my husband, I constantly looked for the reason behind it all. I know, as many of us instinctively feel is true, that we are here on this earth to learn so that we may grow to the evolved beings we are meant to eventually become. However, understanding the lesson while in the midst of it is nearly impossible, since you have to learn it to recognize it. What I now understand, as I stand with it all behind me, is it wasn't all only for the sake of teaching me something, but was always for the sake of Love.

Oh, I did have a major lesson to learn, but not all of it was successful at teaching me that lesson, even though my problems would have likely been much less if I would have allowed it to. Regardless of whether it taught me what I should have learned every step along the way, the result was always for the sake of Love. Realizing this illustrates to me how absolutely true what I was shown in the all-knowingness is, that Love really is the only thing that matters in all the universe. It is so true, that I can now expand that truth to state that everything that happens to any of us, no matter how small or huge it may be, is always for the sake of Love, because Love is ALL that matters.

Every lesson we learn, every trial or tribulation we go through, every person we meet, whether we end up helping them or hurting them, it is all for the sake of Love. That Love may be towards you or towards someone else your experience affects, but one way or another, it is always for Love. The reason for everything, as this chapter is entitled, is LOVE. It is the law of the universe, the Law of Love. That law is based in the fact that Love is all that matters. It is why we exist and in every case it is the only real reason we experience what we go through.

Love's Reason

My life was blessed in so many ways I can't count them, and that went on for some 15 years, ever since I'd turned my life over to Spirit. My sweet angel was spot on, I did experience true happiness, starting right at the 25 year mark she gave. But, it wasn't because Spirit was taking care of me. It was because I was focusing on my LOVE for humanity with every effort to do anything Spirit asked of me, the same Love I felt while within the spiritual realm.

All through those years of misunderstanding why I was so blessed, I was unable to use my own life as an

The Reason For Everything

example of how Love works. It took suffering to turn that around. As soon as my focus left that Love and I stopped writing as my husband grew sicker, my passion for humanity got buried away in my grief. Once all those intentions of Love turned inward and became only about my self-centered loss, all hell broke loose in my life.

Then, when my focus returned to my Love for humanity through writing that book I thought I'd published, my health was back on the right track, and I was feeling stronger than I had in years. But when I thought that book was done, all I had ahead of me was suffering in solitude as I waited for the spiritual promises. I lost hope in ever realizing my destiny, and as a result my health took a very bad turn once again.

We can blame it all on what appears to be whatever random fate chooses to come our way, but what I am trying to illustrate through my example, is that Love is the driving force of our fate. Focusing on Love really does make all your problems go away, and staying focused on Love keeps them away. There really is a reason for everything, and that reason is always for the sake of Love.

What I am trying to say, now that I can use my own life as a perfect example, is what I was shown in the Grand Canyon is the ABSOLUTE TRUTH of MANKIND! It took facing death to wake me up to how it manifests in our physical reality. That focus alone is the only reason I am still alive today. Love really is all that matters and the only lesson we really need to learn. A quick review of the hard times of my life should clearly illustrate what I'm saying. It should help you see how Love played a part in any and all of it.

The Handicapped Widow

The first thing to review is how the universe treated the handicapped widow I became. Our tenants of 8 years left our rental home a complete shambles, unlivable, untenable, and nearly unrepairable. Their departure left me with no income what-so-ever, and expenses way beyond what I'd imagined possible. To understand how Love could be the reason behind all this turmoil, let's think about where I was when this happened.

I was completely alone in my devastation over the loss of my one true Love. With no support structure in place at all, nobody was there to come to comfort me or help me see beyond my grief. There were no kids for me to care for, no work to go to or orders to fill or books to write, since I'd already put all that behind me over a year before.

Where did that leave me? It left me in a dark hole I never would have been able to find my way out of if my income flow had remained intact. If I wouldn't have had something to fight for, I would have had no reason to get out of bed at all. It gave me a purpose, something to work towards, something to force me to take my mind off of my own selfish grief.

It also gave me something to focus my anger on rather than the doctors who betrayed my husband or the constant regrets of those things I wish I would have said or done with my husband. Those are things I could do nothing about, while the problems with my rental house were something I could do something about. It gave me a reason for living beyond waiting for a vision that was not on the horizon.

Where is the purpose of Love in all that? There are actually several ways Love comes into play in this saga. For one thing, there were lessons for the contractors in how they should approach life with compassion in their heart. Whether they learned it or not is their journey, but I know one of them, at least, paid the price for his dishonesty. I informed the online website I found him at and with pictures gave evidence in a review of his devastation. The site kicked him off and he was counting on that site as his sole source for revenue leads. I also know he lost jobs he'd already landed as a result of my review.

Another very important aspect of Love actually came from telling my story. As you read about the con men taking advantage of me, did you feel any compassion in your heart? That is being human and that is Love. Your compassion towards what happened to me added a whole lot of Love to the universe, and that made a huge difference you can't even imagine. You will understand how that works better after reading my next book, *Echoes From Spirit*. Just know for now, that you helped all of humanity by being human and feeling that little bit of compassion as you read my story.

Then, of course, there was Spirit's Love for humanity including me, sending me something to keep me occupied and focused on rather than the loss of my husband. To just leave me alone to wallow in my grief until I faded away and died from a broken heart was not an option, because I still had a job for the sake of Love to do for humanity. People die from broken hearts all the time, and that is definitely where I was headed if I wouldn't have had something to get out of bed and fight for.

You may be wondering why Spirit had to make it so expensive, when it could have still been something I could focus on without it being so overwhelming to my finances. That is actually the beautiful part in all this, the part that is clearly Spirit sent. It turns out, almost all of the costs came out of the money Spirit sent me. It illustrates to me that it all had its purpose in my destiny. There really is a reason for everything, even the bad things.

You see, we didn't have any life insurance at all, since we didn't really believe in insurance. To me, insurance is like asking for trouble. You are putting out to the universe that you expect this horrible thing to happen, so you get insurance to lessen the blow. It's negative thinking in my way of seeing things, inviting disaster.

It was only a few months before my husband died when we started getting these notices in the mail from the VA offering life insurance. I ignored it at first, but then it started to make sense, because I was beginning to realize my husband was not going to recover from his ailments. It was probably on the third such notice that I decided to follow up on it without even telling my husband about it until he had to sign the final paperwork. I didn't want to add that negativity to his thought patterns, but realized the reality was already there and I should do something to protect myself. He was surprised when I asked him to sign the papers, but I think it gave him some comfort too.

It was immediately when the paperwork was done and the insurance was in place, and even before the first premium payment was deducted from my husband's monthly VA benefit, that my husband died. Now if the timing of that isn't Spirit sent, then I don't know what is. It totaled very near to what the expenses of repairing that house came to. Spirit wasn't sending me more than I could handle, and even made sure I could handle it by providing me the means to pay for it. That's Love.

And finally, there is the lesson in Love it all had for me. Even though I failed to learn the primary lesson in Love, which is to Love myself, it taught me forgiveness. Without even noticing it, I now have compassion in my heart even for my enemies. I understand that we all do what our situations in life force us to do, and until I have walked in their shoes, I have no right to judge the actions of others.

We are all just doing our best to get through this life the only way we know how, which is all also for the sake of Love. Everything in life each of us goes through is all designed to teach us how to Love, or what Love is, or to add compassion to the totality of mankind.

Love Vs Death's Door

Even if you can see how Love had something to do with all the corruption of the world having its way with me, you are probably having a hard time seeing how Love could be part of bringing me to the brink of death. Well, first of all, remember, Spirit was answering my own prayer. I had asked for death, because I couldn't face a life of solitude if the spiritual promises weren't going to come through for me. That answer to my prayer even gave me hope that Spirit was still there for me, responding to my requests.

I know that sounds crazy to people who consider life as the ultimate, but I know it's not my first and won't be my last time around this block called life. Human life is nothing more than a short journey out of 100's, maybe even 1000's of similar journeys we've all taken or will take on this earth plane. Death is only the ending of one journey and the beginning of another. Therefore, Spirit was only giving me the option to exit this journey ahead of schedule at my own request. So, from that perspective, Spirit was granting me my wish out of Love and respect for my choices, while at the same time, leaving the door open for me to make a different choice.

Then, of course, there is once again the compassion my story should bring up in others, which is always a component of Love found in every struggle anyone may go through. But the most important aspect of Love in this part of my story is the lesson it finally taught me. Since I couldn't learn it by the corruption being sent my way, Spirit had to send me an even worse struggle.

First and foremost, the experience of tasting death was designed to teach me the important lesson of how to Love myself enough to take responsibility for my own wellbeing. I had so little self-respect that I was allowing the corruption to overwhelm me and the medical professionals to put me into their labeled box I knew I didn't belong in. It was a box that was labeled "death by obesity", and I was fulfilling their prophesy perfectly. I am not that person!! I'm here for a purpose, even my obesity has a purpose, and that purpose is for the Love of humanity. I can't HELP the humanity I Love so much from a grave.

My only way back to good health is to stop believing what they want me to believe, that I need their drugs to survive. I have to take responsibility for finding my own solutions to my problems, my own way of decreasing my inflammation and fluids overload, which I am still working on resolving as I write this. I know absolutely that I don't have some terminal disease, or even any disease, that they may want me to have for their own satisfaction. I now believe the reason my Guru told me I would never contract a disease was to help me find the strength to overcome their diagnosis when this time came. It truly was his words that gave me the confidence to know that I do not belong in their box.

The Reason Is Love

When I say Love is the reason for everything, I mean it is the reason for all the lessons we go through here in this earth school. Most people realize we are here to learn, but they usually don't associate what they've learned with Love, because it's often very subtle or well hidden. I promise you, however, in one way or another, either directly or indirectly, it's always about Love, because LOVE IS ALL THAT MATTERS!!!

Please understand, I am a firsthand witness to this reality of our existence. I saw the world literally from the spiritual perspective, from God's perspective. I know as absolutely as I know my name, not only that Love is all that matters, but why Love matters at all, and even how it makes all the difference in how we experience life. I know the way the universe works scientifically, which I will explain in my next book. But since Love is the primary purpose in all I was shown, it will be the common theme in every book I write.

I realize that I could say those words until my throat closed up, and you still won't hear me. Just like those spirits told me in my hotel room that night, "it's just like it was when Jesus was here". Jesus also told us that it's all about Love, so this is definitely not new information. I fully realize those words are nothing more than empty syllables without a complete understanding of how it all works within the science of our physical realm supported by how our reality manifests from the spiritual perspective. That will all be explained fully in my next book.

I am here to share with you the answers to some of the most mind boggling questions mankind has had since human beings began on this world. It's time to learn why we are here, why does life exist at all, how the universe was created, why do bad things happen to good people, where is God in all this, and even what God actually is among the many other undefined or misunderstood aspects of our reality. First and foremost, I'm here to tell you what Love has to do with any and all of it.

By filling in those blanks for you in the books yet to come, I'm hoping you will be able to fully grasp the truth of

Love and thereby gain control over your own destiny. You see, this is the most important part of the message I have for the general population of mankind, but it's the hardest to communicate in a way that will be beneficial. That message is; Love is the key to our salvation. By that, I mean it is the way out of all our problems, the access to freedom from strife we all deserve.

It saddened me greatly, during my Grand Canyon experience, as I watched all the people of the world suffer in their trivial drama. I could even feel the weight of the fears they carry through life. It troubled me so much, because I knew they didn't have to suffer at all. It was a choice they were making, and they didn't even understand that they were making a choice. It all seemed so simple from the spiritual realm, but I know, and hope you realize I know, that it's not simple from this physical perspective we've surrounded ourselves in.

Even so, here is that message I wanted to shout from the rooftops. YOU DO NOT HAVE TO SUFFER!! It's a CHOICE YOU are making. All you have to do to put your struggle behind you, is MAKE A DIFFERENT CHOICE. The choice you should be making is LOVE, that is all there is to it. Just LOVE ALL THAT IS, and all your torment will come to an end. I guarantee it; this is the absolute truth of the universe. LOVE IS ALL THAT MATTERS!!! It's a universal LAW!

As I said, you should continue reading the books in this series to learn what makes it a law and how the law works, among many more fascinating tidbits of the science of Love and Love energy. I'm even planning on explaining some parts of the Bible people may be curious about, like what Jesus meant when he said we could move mountains or why he washed the feet of his disciples. I have a lot of new and exciting information for the world. I can even answer some of the questions the scientists are currently asking regarding their latest discoveries, new information that defies the long established laws of physics they have actually been forced to put back on the drawing board.

Don't worry though, it won't be any of the controversial stuff, so you don't have to fear that my words may end up stepping on your beliefs. I'm bound by that pact from Spirit, and I will honor that pact until the day I die, or until I receive the vision I was promised I "will receive" that will release me from it. When that day comes, however, all gloves will be off, the bars will be gone, and the door of my prison will be opened wide. I promise you, though, that I will warn people on the outside or first couple pages of that book(s) to inform you that the contents are not meant for those who may not be ready for full disclosure. The thing is, though, if you've read and assimilated all of my books prior, you WILL be ready. THAT is the way Spirit works.

A Call For Help

As before, I have this last chapter to deal with. I still feel the need to be honest and completely forthright with my readers. Here I am preaching how to overcome all your problems, and I'm still struggling with one of the biggest problems mankind can face, recovering from death itself. When a person declines that far, the journey back to health is overwhelming even in the best environment with a loving family providing all the support a person could ask for. That ideal environment is not where I am sitting, which is why this chapter is still necessary, because I need your help if I am going to overcome my struggle. I can't do this alone.

At least I'm on the right track this time. I'm doing my best to be my own advocate, to take responsibility for my own recovery. But, it's not going real well. When my doctor told me my blood test revealed a deficiency in protein, I figured out that the lack of protein supporting my muscles must be where a lot of my overall pain is coming from. However, our kidneys have trouble with handling a lot of protein when they are damaged, so my efforts to increase my protein intake resulted in further kidney failure. Sure enough, the pain did lessen, but the swelling has started to return.

I'm currently trying to find that delicate balance of protein intake and kidney function, so I'm still working at finding my own way to recovery. That's not the kind of help I need from my readers, even though your support through your prayers would be greatly appreciated. The kind of help I need is the help my Guru promised me, and I need your support before that help can come to me. The reason I say this goes back to the messages from Spirit, so let's look at them again from the perspective of my current reality.

Specific Needs

The only hope I have of ever achieving a full recovery from my condition, including my home bound situation, is to lose all this excess water weight I'm carrying around. I've actually gained back all the fluids I lost in the hospital, so I'm probably weighing well over 550 pounds again. This makes any movement very difficult and therefore muscle development unrealistic. If I am unable to improve I will lose the support Medicare is providing soon, which is the threat I am facing every time the Physical Therapist comes. If I lose all PT support, the only thing left will be hospice, since I refuse to let them take me to a nursing home.

All these years I've known in my heart that the help to lose weight promised by my Guru would not be in the form of the normal means of diet and exercise. Now I finally understand why, because the majority of my excess weight is NOT FAT, it's FLUIDS. I've been blaming my thyroid condition for keeping the weight on me, and it is why I couldn't lose the excess fat I do carry. But my weight from fat is not what is killing me. It's not fat that causes my heart congestion or the shortness of breath I'm experiencing with every effort to work out my muscles. If those things are not resolved, I will continue to have difficulty regaining my strength. My primary NEED, therefore, is to lose these fluids permanently.

My Guru's Promise

This brings me to the point I made earlier, regarding what my Guru had told me. He said that I would receive the help to lose enough weight to do what I NEED to do. I'd assumed he meant I'd be able to do what I wanted to do, but I eventually realized that is not what he said. I've wondered all these years what it was I would "need" to do. That need is clear to me now. I NEED to regain my muscle strength literally for the sake of my survival. If that's not a NEED, then I don't know what is. Finally his message is making complete sense.

He also told me it would get a LOT worse before it got better. Back then I was only dealing with weight from fat, and had no idea a person could gain weight from any other means. To me, it was getting worse enough, and so I was constantly looking for that promised help. I repeatedly recruited people who wanted to help me do what I knew in my heart was not the right way for the weight loss to materialize.

They all wanted me to diet and exercise, but I could never put my whole heart into it even as I went through the paces they assigned. I just knew it wasn't going to happen that way, since my thyroid wasn't ready to let any of that weight from fat go. I thought the right person would know what to do when the time came for his promise to be realized, which is why I had to just let it go and leave it up to Spirit for that time to come. That time HAS come, but there is still something that needs to line up before the promise of help can materialize.

My Message From Spirit

Spirit told me both how and when my weight loss would happen. The how was that it would be "as if by a miracle". That always meant to me that it would not only NOT be by diet and exercise, but also that it would probably be a loss of a lot of weight very quickly. For once it appears my assumptions were probably correct. A weight loss of fluids would be very quick, just like it was when I went to the hospital. I lost about 130 pounds over an 11 day period. Match that with any form of normal weight loss.

It also explains why it would be "as if" by a miracle, since obviously it wasn't a miracle. Spirit was just letting me know it would happen very quickly, something that would be far outside the normal speed of weight loss. Even though I never understood how a quick loss of so much weight would be possible, I've felt in my gut from the moment of receiving this message that this was the meaning, as if the gut feeling was also Spirit sent.

With the "need" understood and the method of how it could be "as if by a miracle" a clear possibility, there is only one more component that still needs to line up. The WHEN part of Spirit's message is still not a condition that has been realized, and until it is, the help I so badly need will not come. The message from Spirit was that it would be when "many people will see it". That explains why the conditions were not lined up when I lost the 130 pounds in the hospital. In fact, I never even thought of that weight loss as being the loss I was promised, or even that it was fluids I needed to lose. Perhaps that's because the NEED wasn't in place until now.

You see, I can't repeat that last solution by going back into the hospital, because I had way too much trouble getting out last time. They wanted me to go to a nursing home because I live alone. I had to beg my brother to come once again to my aid. He really did not want to and only stayed for one day, so I was on my own very quickly. I don't have any faith that I would be able to get him here a third time. He'd insist I go to a nursing home too.

After the poor care I got in the hospital brought me very close to gangrene, I have zero confidence that any nursing home would do better. Therefore, returning to the hospital or going to a nursing home is literally a death sentence for me. I'm simply too large for people to want to go through the struggle of cleaning me properly, and "liability issues" stop them from allowing me to go to the bathroom on my own. A slow death from lack of care is just not an option I'm willing to consider. Besides, I have pets and a property to take care of. I'd lose everything even if I did survive.

The One Remaining Condition

With my only hope for survival being the loss of these fluids weighing me down, and the difficulty I am having achieving that on my own, I long for the help my Guru promised me so many years ago. Problem is, there is still that one condition that needs to be in place before that promise can become my reality. The environment has to be present where "many people will see it".

In all these years, there is only one scenario I've been able to think of where this could be a possibility. The success of my book was how I imagined many people would be paying enough attention to me to notice a change in my condition. But the message was they would have to SEE me, so my imagination also added a spot on television, such as maybe the Oprah show. I know, it sounds like another one of those far-fetched pipe dreams.

Believe me, I get it. I know I shouldn't be putting my hopes into something so grandiose as an interview with

Oprah, but that pipe dream has turned from a dream into a need for my very survival. Somehow MANY people have to SEE me or I will not be able to overcome my situation. I need that help promised by my Guru, and Spirit told me it would come when "many people will see it", so I can't help but see it as my only hope of survival.

Begin My Destiny

Not only is the help to lose these fluids from my body needed for my survival, but I also see it as a necessity if I am going to be all Spirit had in mind for me. I can be no help to anyone while it takes everything I've got to just sustain myself. Even sitting upright for writing is difficult, so how will I be able to teach that little girl if she comes to my door? Obviously, the tents and teepees will never show up in my yard, and standing on world stages to share my "work" is completely impossible.

Once the first two books of this series are published, I will have fulfilled my one promise to the best of my ability, which was to share what I was shown in the all-knowingness with the world. I know I can finally articulate that in a way that everyone will be able to understand, so I will remain determined to achieve that goal regardless of the struggle in getting there. But, whether or not I go beyond that effort will depend on how these books are received by the world.

Let's face it, I'm completely alone and am forced to remain alone by my inability to leave my home, so the life I'm fighting for really isn't worth all this pain and effort. There is only one thing that would make it worth it for me; only one hope that keeps me going, that humanity can learn from my struggle. It's all I have left in the world, my one and only reason for living, to help humanity with what I'm here to teach the world.

I've told you repeatedly, that all you have to do is Love all that is to make all your problems fade away and be gone. So then, if that's the premise of what I'm here to teach, how can I publish any book without overcoming my condition first to be that example for my readers? This is the thing; I'm doing what I know I have to do, which is to tell the world the truth I was shown of our reality. The only way I can be an example of that truth, however, will come "when many people can see it".

Remember that first message I got as well, the one telling me why I had to use my real name rather than hide behind an alias. Spirit told me the "many" people have to "see you to believe it". That tells me this is all part of the plan for my life. I don't know how it will all manifest, or what the "help" I'm waiting for will even look like. All I know is what Spirit told me, which is that many people have to see me for them to believe what I'm here to say, and what they will see is a weight loss that will appear to be as if it happened by a miracle.

All I can do in the meantime is continue the wait for the promises from Spirit to manifest while I do my best to remain focused on my Love for mankind. The answer to finding the way out of any struggle is in staying focused on the desired result based on Love rather than in the struggle getting there. The race can only be won by placing one foot in front of the other. It's up to the universe to cause our opponents to trip or our hurdles to be brought lower to the ground. Our job is to simply stay focused on that sensation of crossing the finish line with our arms spread wide to make way for the yellow ribbon to break across our chest as we cross over.

The finish line for me is the completion of these first two books I am writing. Publishing this work is my only way of placing that foot in front of the other. The only hope I have to cling to, is that everything does happen for a reason, and all those spiritual experiences, visions, messages, and miracles were not for nothing. My trust that Spirit has a plan in this too is keeping me going long enough to put my foot out there for the world to see. My Love for humanity is the only focus I have to cling to and the only visible light I can reach for. We won't see the results of my Love until the effort can come to fruition with all the conditions in place.

Another Scenario

It's been a couple months now that I've been struggling to survive while allowing my body to fix itself. I'm avoiding all drugs and even coffee in my attempt to keep my kidneys functioning fully, but it's not working very well. Even having too much protein is causing my kidneys to slow down in the healing process, so keeping them at full capacity has been fruitless for the most part. In the meantime I've been forced to sleep in my electric lift chair recliner because of the constant trips to the bathroom, since my bed is just too difficult for me to get in and out of so many times a night, which is at least every two hours.

Even though my ankles have gone down by about a centimeter (less than ½ inch), I just discovered tonight that my thighs are starting to leak fluids through the skin. That is where this all began, except this is worse, since I can't bandage my thighs. In fact, it's what has motivated me to force myself to finish this book tonight. This struggle is so difficult that I don't know for sure that I'm going to make it this time, so I have to fulfill my promise to Spirit while I still can. I have to tell my vision of truth to the world before I can no longer speak.

Regardless of what happens to me next, there is one thing I know for sure. I know the world will hear my truth eventually, even if it is too late for me to receive the rewards I long for. I know this because of some more messages from Spirit I haven't told you about yet, both

The Reason For Everything

through my Indian Grandmother and other psychics I've pursued since. It is because of these messages that I feel so driven to close this book on such a sour note. Sorry about that, but it is another part of my spiritual journey I can't leave unsaid.

The first time I heard this message, it came from my Indian Grandmother, whom I feel very confident was clearly in touch with Spirit and someone I know I can trust fully. She said Spirit was giving her a message she needed to pass on to me, that people won't hear the information I'm here to share until after I die. She said she could see people talking about it, and could hear them saying, "that's exactly what that lady said in her book". She even laughed at the scene of them smiling and carrying on about how I was right all along. But none of that will happen until after I have passed on from this world.

Similar messages came from 2 local psychics I've spoken to since, who informed me that the message of my work won't be heard until after my death, but without any further details. I didn't need clarification anyway, since I'd already heard that news. Where that information leaves me, however, is wondering if I will overcome my current health issues, or will they continue to overwhelm me beyond my ability to continue the fight.

So you see, that is one scenario I do have to face and why I have to write this chapter. I can hope those messages were referring to the scientists not hearing me rather than the entire world closing their ears, but I don't know and they didn't clarify. Perhaps that is even why my promises from Spirit haven't materialized yet, because they are dependent on whether the humanity I Love so much is ready to hear me or wants to hear more.

Like I said, predestiny is better thought of as a predisposition, because our free will is the one in charge.

Vision Of Truth

Since my only true motivation, the only thing I sincerely CARE about, is focused on my Love for the rest of mankind rather than Loved ones in my own life, it means my destiny depends on the free will of the humanity I so badly want to help. If that Love cannot be received by even a few, then the disposition of my predestiny is that I was ahead of my time, too early to be helpful during my lifetime.

That is what I am so moved to tell my readers before I can no longer speak. That I cannot promise I will remain long enough to expand further on what I have been able to share here or teach all I've learned over those many years of research, because it's not up to me, it's up to YOU. I will do my best to continue to fight as long as I can, but I need the help of my readers to set the stage for that promise of help to materialize. I need enough people looking my way for the condition of "many people will see it" to exist.

My Last Hope

What I am asking for is your help in getting the word out that this book even exists. Let's face it, I'm a 61 year old widow with no children or grandchildren keeping me up-to-date on the latest technology. I have a Facebook account, but I don't use it, and since it was hacked I've placed the highest securities on it and removed my one photo. I did establish a website, Eagle-Awareness.com, but I don't know how to do anything else in the massive social media game going on these days. To tell you the truth, my daily struggle is making even finishing this first book very difficult, so I don't know what else I will be able to achieve. It will take all I have to complete my next and what could be my final book.

Worse yet, I won't be able to go to any radio stations for interviews or go meet my fans at bookstores for book signings in my home bound condition. Even a plea to Oprah or any possible television spots are out of the question without the marketing in place to grab their attention. They would have to come to me, and they are not going to do that for some unknown, unread, first time author whose books aren't even being read.

Marketing is everything, and I cannot possibly achieve it on my own without help in my condition, not even a little bit. What I am saying, readers, is I need your help on that front. I need YOUR compassion for humanity, or at least for me, to make this book a success enough for the "many people" to see it so that the help I need to survive will come.

Writing this book is all I can do from the living room of my beautiful property, but it's my hope that it will be the catalyst that opens the door to the spiritual life I long for. I just can't promise my readers something I can only hope will be the outcome, because it depends on my readers, not on Spirit and not on me. I have to be real, this book may not be considered good enough to entice readers to pass it on to their friends or spread the word to others so it can become successful. The world may still not be ready for what I am here to share.

Unless the release of the new information described in my next book, *Echoes From Spirit*, leads me to whatever my next step to help humanity is meant to be, then my journey is over at this point right now. This is the certainty I'm residing in, the realization that my future potentials are radically dependent on how this information, my vision of truth, is received by the world, by YOU.

Understand me, please, when I say it doesn't really matter to me. It's not my intention to put undo stress or undeserved responsibility on my readers for my survival. It's actually okay with me either way, because I have no fear of death, since I believe I've already seen a sample of the other side and it sure looks good to me. As long as I can get these first two books out there, then I know my words will be heard eventually, and I know I did my very best to do what I could for my Love towards all that is. I can expect no more from myself and I know Spirit won't begrudge me for my efforts.

If this is my first and my last word to the world, at least I won't leave this world a failure. I will have achieved what I came here to achieve, because one thing is sure, these first 2 books will be published, and soon. But whether or when the public will pick them up to read what I'm here to say is out of my control. I just know that if it is out there somewhere, it will be heard eventually just as surely as that invitation to the Australian Vietnam Veterans Celebration found our meek abode of less than a month. When it's meant to be, it will be, and I know for sure, this information is meant to be delivered to humanity, and it is meant to be delivered by me once humanity is ready to hear me.

What I am trying to say with this long winded reality check, is that I know absolutely that what I've said here is true, that Love is all that matters, and the science and reality behind how and why is also true, which I will be explaining in my next book, *Echoes From Spirit*. I just can't promise I will be able to remain as an example of that truth. Even though my faith in the promises from Spirit of my own future destiny of helping humanity has grown weak, there is nothing in this world that can shake my knowing that what I'm here to share is the absolute reality of mankind.

I have good days, where my hope and faith in Spirit coming through for me remain strong, and I have bad days, where the pain makes the future look pretty bleak. The thing is, though, my situation is extremely rare, since most people have someone who Loves them enough to give them the hope they need to carry on. With the support of your Loved ones, you can find the purpose that will fulfill you and that purpose in Love will cause your problems to disappear from your life. I promise you, it is the LAW!

It's not that my Love for humanity won't turn my life around for me. I continue in my faith that it will, and it already has helped me reach beyond death to this point. It's just that I'm in the latter years of my life in a condition that cannot continue without that purpose of Love sustaining me, and that purpose depends on whether mankind is ready for my message. If those promises and predictions from spiritual sources don't come through, because the world doesn't want to hear from me, then my efforts to help humanity will die here and I will die with them and without the world ever knowing me.

With that said, and the understanding that you may not be reading this until after that day when my existence on this earth came to an end, let me just say this in closing. You've most likely missed something very important, if this is the first time you've heard of me or my message for the world. Because I do still have faith that everything happens for a reason, which means I did NOT have all those wondrous spiritual experiences or receive all those astounding spiritual messages for nothing. I'm confident that the help did come and I did achieve spiritual success before I passed on.

In other words, if I am gone from this world as you are reading this, then there is a little girl out there, now likely a grown woman approaching her later years, whom I opened my heart to completely and taught her all I know, which reaches far beyond the message of these books. Seek HER out, for she has a very important job for the world, and will help you see the truth of these words and much more.

WITH ALL MY LOVE FOR ALL THAT IS, be proud to be the divine human being you are! Be thankful, because LOVE

IS ALL THAT MATTERS!! If you want the proof of that, and the science that backs it up, then please start looking for my next book, *Echoes From Spirit*, where the complete depth of what I was shown in the all-knowingness is explained in full.

With my situation disclosed and my spiritual journey detailed for the world to see, it's time I get busy with my next and what may be my final book. It's time for me to fulfill the promise I made to Spirit all those many years ago. As those readers from that small psychic fair told me to do, and after well over 4 decades since I promised I would, it's time I finally GO FOR IT!!

References

For access to the vast knowledge passed down to us by Kryon, you can visit Lee Carroll's site at: http://www.kryon.com

For more information or to order the book A Course In Miracles, you can visit their website: http://www.acim.org

For more information on the reincarnation study by Dr. Ian Stevenson, visit the website: http://www.reluctant-messenger.com/reincarnation-proof.htm

For more information on the reincarnation study by Jim B. Tucker, visit the website: www.uvamagazine.org/articles/the_science_of_reincarnation

To learn more about me or about the Eagle Awareness Program or to give me your feedback on what you would like to see at a spiritual retreat, please visit: http://www.eagle-awareness.com

To have a closer look at the CALLIGRAPHY the homeless stranger drew, whether out of curiosity or to help solve its mystery, please visit: http://www.eagle-awareness.com

The dictionary used to look up a couple words was a two volume Funk & Wagnall's Standard Desk Dictionary, which was part of a set of encyclopedias, the 1980 edition.

www.ingramcontent.com/pod-product-compliance
Lightning Source LLC
Chambersburg PA
CBHW071309110426
42743CB00042B/1233